NEW DECORATED GARDEN

NEW DECORATED GARDEN

transform your outside space into a haven of

calm and tranquility

elspeth thompson　　melanie eclare

CICO BOOKS

LONDON　NEW YORK

This edition published in 2020 by CICO Books

An imprint of Ryland Peters & Small Ltd

20–21 Jockey's Fields   341 E 116th St

London WC1R 4BW   New York, NY 10029

www.rylandpeters.com

10 9 8 7 6 5 4 3 2 1

First published in 2002

Text © Elspeth Thompson 2002

Design and photography © CICO Books 2002, 2020

A CIP catalog record for this book is
available from the Library of Congress and
the British Library.

ISBN: 978 1 78249 816 2

Printed in China

Photographer: Melanie Eclare
Editor: Clare Double
Art director: Sally Powell
Production controller: David Hearn
Publishing manager: Penny Craig
Publisher: Cindy Richards

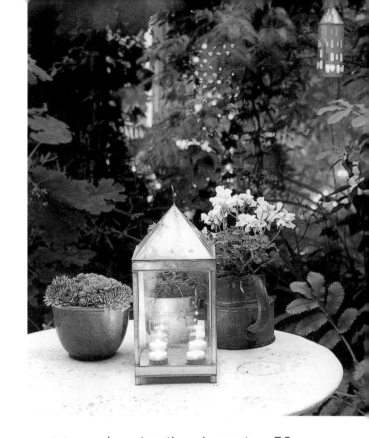

contents

introduction   6

part one: choosing a style   8

city haven   10

mediterranean color   16

modern formal   22

exotic illusion   28

enchanting spaces   34

sensual minimalism   40

naturally dynamic   46

part two: choosing the elements   52

furniture   54

lighting   66

art and sculpture   76

containers   88

decorative plant supports   100

topiary   106

summerhouses and retreats   112

water features   118

groundworks   124

directory   138

picture credits   140

index   142

acknowledgments   144

introduction

Modern gardens are more than a motley collection of plants around a lawn. These days, our outside spaces are as likely to contain furniture, sculpture, lighting, and heating as any room inside—some may even have a fireplace, a hot tub, or a place to work or sleep. We are familiar with the notion of the outdoor room, but this is not just a matter of moving furniture outside. In recent years, our whole sense of style has leaped the bounds of the house to define the yard as new ground for personal expression. Trees and plants combine with all the other decorative elements to create individual outdoor worlds—well-designed custom-made spaces in which children can play, adults can entertain, family and friends can relax, socialize, read, meditate, or do nothing at all.

The new decorated garden is a personal and practical reflection of the gardener's life, style, and vision. Sometimes, as in the penthouse roof terrace featured in this book, the colors and materials used indoors are continued outside, creating a seamless transition between interior and exterior. At other times—and the extraordinary exotic garden of a Los Angeles set designer is an example—the garden becomes a world of its own, filled with finds from a lifetime of travel and collecting. Tiny town gardens can be transformed into intimate outdoor dining rooms, flickering with

candle flames and tree lights, or furnished with built-in sofas, silk awnings, and brightly colored cushions. A fire is lit in the hearth, a fountain begins to bubble, and the scene is set for an enchanted evening under the stars.

Art and sculpture can join hands with nature to create gardens as rich in poetry and association as they are in visual style. Whether commissions for a particular corner of the garden, gallery purchases, or original *objets trouvés*, they provide focus for the mind as well as the eye. Where the vision is strong enough, one grand artistic gesture—such as the S-shaped dry-laid stone wall that snakes its way through a suburban garden featured in these pages—can lift the garden itself into the realms of abstract art.

All aspects of the garden provide scope for individual artistic expression, from the choice of materials for flooring, paths, and walls to water features and lighting. Think of them all as elements that will add to the garden's finished feel and style. Even outdoor furniture is more than just a case of going shopping. Modern designs can be mixed with old; salvage can be found a new home and antiques upholstered in unusual fabrics or given a lick of unexpected paint. Interesting found objects can be integrated into the garden, transformed into one-of-a-kind tables, plant tubs, and wind chimes. A summerhouse or treehouse can be furnished as a romantic dining room or secret personal den. Water can be played against frosted glass or trickled down a cairn of stones to make a sensual moving sculpture.

Good gardens are naturally more than a collection of furniture, materials, and objects, however beautiful these might be. They are a subtle partnership between hard landscaping, decorative elements, and the all-important plants. After all, what is the point of outside living, if not to appreciate the seasonal changes of flowers and foliage, as well as the weather? Gardens with too few plants in them just don't feel like gardens at all. In each of the gardens featured in this book, decoration never upstages nature: rather, it works alongside the plants to create a perfect setting for outdoor living in its broadest sense. These are places of passionate and personal inspiration, well able to adapt to the demands of modern life—a venue for a party one day, the next a peaceful haven where the cares of the world can be forgotten in the splash of water on stone. But they also leave room for nature's own artistry—for the sudden dappled shadows of leaves on a lawn or the surreal pink snowfall of cherry blossoms in spring.

part one

choosing a style

city haven **10**

mediterranean color **16**

modern formal **22**

exotic illusion **28**

enchanting spaces **34**

sensual minimalism **40**

naturally dynamic **46**

city haven

Simple shapes, urban textures, and big bold planting transform a tiny concrete patio in a city center into a delightful haven for meditation or entertaining—and a mirror opens up the space.

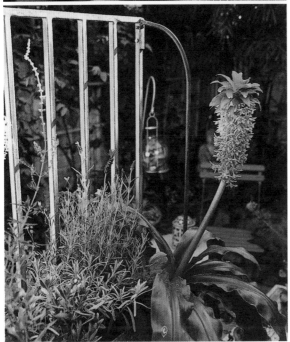

Main picture: The brick raised beds hold objects such as a plaster Buddha and metal lanterns that can be moved around the garden.

Top: The garden seen through the French doors, showing the metal grillwork bridging the basement well. Note the climbers trained along wires above—white mini lights twinkle among the foliage at night.

Above: Galvanized metal was also used for the modern balustrading, which incorporates a rectangular planting trough.

The tiny garden nearly stopped me from buying our London house. Twenty by twenty feet (six by six meters) of bare painted concrete with a high wall on three sides, it was not the dream plot I'd been waiting for. But I could see how, with work and imagination, this little yard could fit in with the way I like to live: in one large fluid space, with a lot of interaction between inside and out. If we knocked the whole of the ground floor into one big room for living, cooking, eating, and entertaining in, and turned a double-hung window into tall double doors, the garden could become a leafy outside extension to this space.

The first job was to paint the walls white and erect chunky trellis for training climbers—I envisaged a "wallpaper" effect of leaves, flowers, and shadows against a white background. The next problem was to bridge the gap over the basement window well that opened immediately outside the French doors. Pieces of galvanized metal grillwork were sturdy, while still letting in light downstairs. They also suited the urban aesthetic: I've never been keen on cottage gardens in the city. Salvaged scaffold planks made a strong square deck on the upper level, while narrower wood was used for two smaller, lower decks. I painted the wood white with thinned-down latex—it needs renewing every spring, but this doesn't take long, and perks the place up for summer. The garden has evolved as a series of squares—from the different-sized decks and the painted table (made from a wooden pallet) to the gaps in the trellis and galvanized grillwork. This, and confining my palette to a few colors and materials—whitewashed wood, yellow London brick, and gray galvanized metal—unifies the space and provides a simple backdrop for the more complex shapes and textures of the plants.

I'm a great believer in large plants in small spaces. Somehow, like large pieces of furniture in tiny rooms, they look exciting and dramatic rather than cramped, and draw

Below: A junk-shop metal table painted white is a good spot for breakfast on the sunny upper deck. The plants behind it are often in total shade, so the addition of a large mirror, installed in a shallow alcove in the back wall, gave the entire garden a new lease on life. In addition to reflecting more light into the bed, it brings a convincing illusion of more space. More galvanized tin lanterns sit on the table and hang from the branches of a winter-flowering cherry, while mismatched folding chairs painted purple and chartreuse complement the colors of the planting.

the eye up to the sky. My main bed contains a large bamboo, a strappy bronze phormium, euphorbias, the candelabra blooms of acanthus, and buff-pink plumes of *Macleaya cordata*, as well as a winter-flowering cherry tree. Sun-loving plants and vegetables grow in old metal vats and trash cans against the south-facing house wall.

Small dimensions concentrate the mind when designing. You have to make choices: if there's only one patch of sun, do you keep it for sitting in or devote it to plants? And there's only room for one style and a simple color scheme. My plants are green, white, silver, purple, and chartreuse, though I enjoy the occasional splash of red or orange, often provided by self-sown nasturtiums. I make changes with the pots and containers near the French doors, moving new plants to center stage as they come into their prime. It also pays to give things several uses: for instance, the brick edge on the raised beds is wide enough to sit on. Eight people

Below: A metalworker was commissioned to make an arch for climbers around the French doors, with a built-in trough filled with silver-gray foliage plants including lavender, perovskia, and *Convolvulus cneorum*. Clematis and morning glory climb the arch (glimpsed on left) from a shiny metal trash can, while a pot containing the pineapple lily, *Eucomis bicolor*, is moved to center stage when it is coming into bloom.

can sit happily around the little table to eat on summer evenings, when the garden is illuminated by electric uplighters and metal lanterns. But probably the biggest impact you can make on a tiny garden is to install a mirror. Mounting six by six feet (two by two meters) of mirror from an old closet into an alcove in the back wall not only increased the amount of light that bounces into the garden; it seems to bring in air and space as well. I knew it had worked when a first-time visitor pointed to the reflection and asked, "So is that your garden through there as well?"

Candles and tree lights create a magical atmosphere after dark, with lanterns grouped on tables as they would be inside.

Left: Votive candles are lit in a lantern from India and tea glasses from Morocco.

Far left: More votives in the base of a huge aluminum bowl that was a present from a friend.

Above: The glowing light and flickering shadows from this collection of makeshift lanterns bring plenty of light to the central area around the table, while electric uplighters at the back of the beds throw shadows of the foliage up the walls. This is a great place for a summer supper outside or for people to flow into during a party—the steps and retaining walls double as extra seating.

mediterranean color

Inspired by Spanish gardens, the brightly painted walls, comfortable chairs, open fireplace, and lily-pond jacuzzi in this small Los Angeles courtyard create the ideal environment for outdoor entertaining.

Courtyard gardens have a long history in hot countries: the high walls provide shade, as does a roofed or loggia area, and the centerpiece is often water, to cool and humidify the air. Nancy Goslee Power has all this and more in her California garden. In just a few years, the interior designer-turned-landscape architect has transformed an unprepossessing backyard into a colorful environment for year-round outdoor living.

The covered section works as a splendid outside living room, with comfortable chairs pulled up around a simple raised fireplace. The hearth provides a focal point, as well as warmth on colder days or when the temperature suddenly drops at night. Another area is devoted to dining,

Main picture: The front yard, which gets the morning sun, is a breakfast terrace, with a geometric floor fashioned from three different shades of stone.

Above left: A painted wooden door leads around the side of the house to the backyard. Even this shady unprepossessing corridor has been transformed by means of a pebble mosaic floor, bright yellow walls, and shade-loving plants.

Above: A long pool is the focal point of the backyard. The rear part is a blue-tiled jacuzzi with built-in seats—perfect for a nighttime soak beneath the stars.

with a mosaic-top table in the shade of large king palms, and a built-in sofa for lounging. The centerpiece of the garden is the long rectangular pool with a fountain trickling from the blue rear wall. Though it looks purely decorative, abloom with water lilies and flag iris, the pool has other, unexpected uses. The near end has been divided off to make a lily pond, which helps to cool and humidify the air by day. And when night falls, the far end becomes a secluded jacuzzi at the flick of a switch, complete with stepped seating and underwater lighting showing off the cobalt-blue lining.

Rigorous planning was vital to fit so much into a relatively small space. With the help of architect Bill Nicholas, Nancy divided the sections to be defined by low shuttered concrete walls. The flooring is of pinkish local stone in an irregular tiled effect—this suits the indoor–outdoor feel and unifies the space. When the bones of the design were in place, she could then have fun with color. The orange of the loggia wall, inspired by a trip to Morocco, was achieved by mixing saffron strands in with the paint. The pink is the soft tone of fresh plaster, while the rich yellow was copied from a building in Brazil. Cushions on chairs and sofa are in stronger shades of purple, pink, and green, and Nancy likes to pick these hues out in her planting, choosing a different pair of colors each year—deep blue agapanthus, for instance, with lime green nicotiana, or perhaps some bright pink 'Star Gazer' lilies—for the pots of flowering plants that she dots around the loggia and pool. Paint, fabric, and plants can be changed relatively easily to create a completely different look from year to year.

One of the joys of this garden is that it works as well with one person, two or three, or a large party. As the retaining walls of beds and pool double as seating, you don't need more chairs to entertain a crowd.

Built-in seating was planned as part of this yard from the outset—pillows in brightly colored textiles furnish this simple sofa and tie in with the colors of potted plants that change annually. The rich yellow of the walls was inspired by a building in Brazil.

One of the joys of this garden is that it works as well with one person, two or three, or a large party. As the retaining walls of beds and pool are wide enough to double as seating, you don't need more chairs to entertain a crowd. And the living room feels cozy if you are alone, with the raised fire glowing at night and candles flickering along the built-in shelf in front.

Nancy's design skills were really put to the test for the more tricky areas of the garden: the small front yard and the dark dingy side yard corridor on one side of the house. A hedge for privacy and a mosaic floor in three different colors of stone have transformed the front yard into a sunny yet secluded spot for breakfast. A built-in raised square bed was created for a small *Metrosideros excelsus* tree at one end of this area. The corridor has been transformed with a wonderful pattern of pebbles underfoot, clever planting, and a coat of bright yellow paint, that creates a convincing illusion of sunshine, whatever the weather.

Above: Large palms (**left**) make a shady canopy above the table, while potted plants (**right**) create a further splash of color. Bright flowering climbers grow overhead.

Opposite above left: The loggia outside the house has been turned into a true outdoor living room complete with a fireplace, comfy armchairs, and candle chandelier hanging from the rafters. The walls are washed orange and pale plaster pink, while the far side is open to the garden.

Opposite above right and below left: Bowls of ornamental gourds stand on a wooden table, while potted plants and other objects are ranged along ledges and the shelf in front of the raised fireplace.

Opposite below right: The colorful dining area has a built-in sofa piled with bright pillows and reddish chairs around a lime-green mosaic table—both paint and pillows can be changed easily.

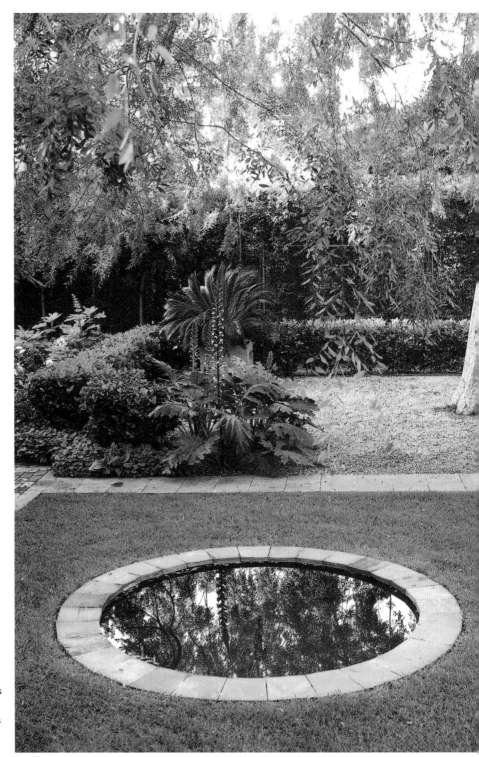

Right: A large Chinese elm encloses much of the garden within its leafy canopy, casting dappled shadows on gravel, grass, and stone. If the close-clipped lawn is like a green carpet, the pool is like a round mirror, reflecting the patterns of branches against the sky. Like other elements in the design, the planting has been kept simple, in different green shades.

Far right: Acanthus, sago palms, and other sculptural foliage plants are grouped beneath the tree while elsewhere, other evergreens have been pruned into low cubes and mounds.

modern formal

Calm geometry and top-quality materials create a mood of restrained elegance in this modern American garden, while its asymmetrical layout and sculptural planting put a contemporary spin on tradition.

Like a well-cut suit or neutrally decorated room, a strong garden layout using quality materials creates a backdrop that can be dressed up or down at will. This garden in a suburb of Los Angeles has the quiet elegance of a Parisian park, with the seasonal patterns of light and shade shifting across squares of paving, pale gravel, and grass. Gaps in the planting frame views through to the bluestone swimming pool and formal potager beyond.

Formal plans based on geometry have a firm footing in the past, but while grand historic gardens were essentially flat affairs devised to be admired from above, today's versions are dynamic, three-dimensional designs for living in. Contrasting materials can be used to denote areas for different uses, while plants are not just employed to make decorative patterns, but to define structure and enclose space. Symmetry may play a part, but old rules are there for breaking. This style interprets traditional design ideas and gives them a contemporary twist.

The starting points for this garden were the large Chinese elm that dominates the main body of the garden, and a pile of pinkish bricks left over from remodeling the back of the house. To connect the garden with the house, which belongs to interior designer Suzanne Rheinstein and her husband, the landscape architect Judy Norton created a series of linked terraces aligned to the view from the library window. Bluestone was laid in a cross pattern with the brick to create small paved

squares that can be used for seating or entertaining or as a site for potted plants. Creamy gravel surrounds the tree, whose graceful arching branches enclose the space like a high vaulted ceiling, providing welcome shade in summer. The close-clipped lawn, surrounded and dissected by narrow stone pathways, works like a glorious green carpet, and just off-center, a perfect round pool mirrors the filigree pattern of branches against the sky.

One of the key features of this garden is restraint. Hard materials are confined to just a few textures and colors, and the standard of finish is high. The simple formal shapes provide a foil for the stunning organic shapes of the plants: while low boxwood hedges repeat the geometry of the lawn in three-dimensional form, the scrolling leaves of acanthus and sago palms are like living sculptures. Essentially this is a green and white garden, with silver foliage and white flowers contrasting with darker evergreens, but the color scheme can be zipped up with temporary plantings in orange, chartreuse, or dark red. The bright paisley leaves of coleus and begonias look great in lime-green-painted planters, while urns spilling over with spidery dark aeoniums and other succulents sound a more classical note.

Hard materials are limited to creamy gravel beneath the tree, bluestone, and pinkish brick that was left over from renovating the house. The bluestone has been used to edge the pond and create narrow paths across the lawn (**far left**), and there are small square terraces with a criss-cross pattern against the pink brick where they intersect (**right**). The occasional splash of color in the form of a brightly painted container or foliage plant (**left**) interrupts this essentially green and white garden.

Like vases of flowers in a minimalist room, pots and containers provide a more decorative element amid the low-key architectural restraint. They are an easy way to bring bright color and seasonal change to the garden—in cooler climates, tender plants would have to move inside in winter.

Left: Perched high on a pedestal, black-red *Aeonium arboreum* 'Schwartzkopf' rises from a cushion of small-leaved succulents in an ornamental urn.

Above: A huge earthenware urn is a strong enough presence without any planting needed to form the centerpiece of the ornamental potager.

Right: The paisley leaves of coleus create a bold effect in this painted wooden planter where the two paths intersect.

Far right: Elsewhere, evergreen and silver-leaved plants are arranged in an abstract three-dimensional collage of clipped spheres, cubes, and mounds.

Essentially this is a green and white garden, but the color scheme can be zipped up with temporary plantings in orange, chartreuse, or dark red.

Crucially, the designer has not been afraid of empty spaces. Like "whitespace" around pictures in a magazine, they impart an air of cool, classic style that can so easily be crowded out. An expanse of well-tended lawn or unadorned paving is a horticultural breath of fresh air—a welcome respite after areas of intense planting. It allows space for the rhythms of nature to play their part in the garden's design, casting long striped evening shadows, or dropping an impromptu mosaic of petals on the grass.

exotic illusion

Trophies from foreign travels join hands with junkyard and dumpster finds to create this intensely personal world full of shrinelike rooms and sculptures—an exotic paradise beyond time and place.

If you're tempted to choose a theme when decorating a garden, it's best to choose one strong idea and go for it big time. This is what the late set designer Tony Duquette and his wife Elizabeth did at their home high in the canyons of Beverly Hills. To step out of the back door is to enter a secret Shangri-La. Gilded temples, shrinelike pavilions, and rickety pagodas are linked by a network of raised walkways and latticed passageways to create the effect of a magnificent ruin deep in the jungle—an exotic world that inhabits an imaginary time and place.

Main picture: The Duquettes met the challenge of this plunging canyon plot by designing a Shangri-La of temples and outdoor living places linked by suspended walkways. The breadth of vision in the garden's creation makes it appear much larger, older, and more exotic than it is.

Left and above: Some of the building materials and sculptures have been cobbled together from salvaged junk. Others, such as this statue, whose inscrutable features are framed by spidery foliage, are treasured finds from faraway places.

Huge palms and eucalyptus trees tower like giant parasols overhead and cast dappled shadows; ferns sprout from weathered walls, and ivy clothes the tree trunks and snakes around doors. Potted ferns and spider plants dangle like leafy chandeliers.

This is a place full of surprises and illusion. While the effects may be larger than life, the garden is not actually very big. Faced with a plot that took in a deep ravine falling steeply away from the house, the Duquettes created a vertical garden, using the height of the established trees to construct a series of linked walkways and garden buildings in between. Neither is the garden nearly as grand as it appears: much of it was achieved on a shoestring with enormous vision and ingenuity. The sculptures and pagodas, for instance, are made from sections of industrial metal lampshades, car headlights, and painted plastic, while what look like carved and gilded pillars are often wooden posts wrapped with gold-embroidered sari fabric and coated in marine varnish. Many of the larger structures

Main picture: The dining pavilion is one of many garden buildings that push up through the vegetation like relics from some forgotten city. Its interior is shaded and intimate, with antique painted shutters framing views out over the garden.

Above left: A battered balustrade from Falcon's Lair, one-time home of Rudolph Valentino, leads to a wooden summerhouse at the bottom of the garden.

Above right: A pair of iridescent obelisks are made from fragments of abalone shell glued to metal frames. The curvaceous totem sculpture beyond is another ingenious salvage creation, concocted from scraps of painted plastic and metal.

Above: A spiny porcupine sculpture guards a summerhouse.

Above right: The garden is an exercise in the ingenious use of salvage. The columns supporting this tiny temple look like gilded carved wood from a distance, but closer inspection reveals them to be covered in sari fabric secured with staples and a coat of shiny marine varnish.

Right: A painted pagoda stands sentinel outside a doorway.

Left: Potted spider plants are like the capitals on columns flanking this walkway—others hang from the ceiling like leafy chandeliers.

Painting the main elements in the garden in a color scheme of red and green was a clever way to bring unity to the diverse and eccentric collection of buildings and sculptures. The paint is now somewhat peeling and faded—combined with the luxuriant foliage which seems to sprout from every surface, this helps to create a convincing illusion of age. The other unifying factor, of course, is the broadly exotic theme.

incorporate salvage from a naval auction: the bridges are cast-off gangplanks, while perforated plastic panels are painted green to look like carved jade walls. Using salvaged trash with such wit and style gives the garden a sense of fun that saves it from pomposity. And painting it all just two colors—green and red, now somewhat faded—was crucial to create unity. Among all this, the few pieces of genuine exotica—Chinese pots, Balinese balls, temple doors, and pediments from Thai houses—can stand out like the treasures they really are. The foliage draws it all together like the threads of an embroidery.

Plants play natural second fiddle to the buildings here, but are used in stylish profusion to furnish the garden and enhance its effects. Huge palms and eucalyptus trees tower like giant parasols overhead and cast soothing dappled shadows; ferns sprout from weathered walls, and ivy clothes the tree trunks and snakes around doors. Potted ferns and spider plants dangle from ceilings like leafy chandeliers, or crown pedestals that flank the entrance to the pool or other parts of the garden. In a place so full of hard landscaping and structure, foliage helps soften the architectural lines and impart a vital air of age and permanence. Orchids, bromeliads, flowering cacti, and agaves function almost as living sculptures in the outdoor rooms, and contribute further to the exotic ambience.

Choosing a strong theme such as this for a garden can provide the focus for a lifetime of collecting. This place is the fruit of more than forty years of work and travel—a repository for finds from all over the world. Even if your ambitions are on a somewhat smaller scale, this approach can create an intensely personal garden, as rich with memories of people and places as it is in atmosphere.

Above and right: In summer, climbing roses bring a flush of pink to the garden, but for much of the rest of the year, color comes from the clever use of paint. The back of the house has been painted soft ocher yellow, with the window frames picked out in powder blue—a combination reminiscent of the Mediterranean. The trellis is also pale blue, while an old folding chair has a coat of buttercup yellow—a bold statement that lifts the other soft pastel colors beyond conventional prettiness.

enchanting spaces

Secrecy and illusion abound in this enchanting garden, filled with mysterious mirrors, twisted topiary trees, and hidden seats for sun and shade at different times of day.

Above: A pointed wooden arch frames the entrance to the main part of the garden, while also providing support for clematis and other climbers. The cobblestone and brick path narrows slightly and almost imperceptibly along its length, making the long narrow garden appear even longer than it is. This is just one of the many ingenious illusory touches employed in this garden—where it ends, a false door set in the wall gives the impression there is a further, secret space beyond.

Some gardens have an atmosphere that enchants and beguiles from the moment you set foot in them. The writer Mirabel Osler has achieved this sort of magic at her home on the border between England and Wales, transforming a narrow urban plot into a delightful world that charms visitors into staying far longer than they'd intended.

Entrances are crucial in creating a sense of magic. This garden is first glimpsed at the far end of a long paved corridor that leads from Mirabel's front door—the view framed in the far doorway entices you in. To pass

Below: Straw hats and wicker baskets arranged in the rear window look attractive from inside and out—an original touch that holds the promise of summer even in the cold winter months. The beautiful climbing rose 'Noisette Carnée' frames the window with a cascade of pale pink blooms and perfectly complements the colors of the house. The Victorian water pump no longer works, but remains an attractive feature.

This garden is made for wandering—and wondering. For such a small space, it has a remarkable array of places to sit and think and watch the wind in the trees. The magic is that each is distinct and entire in itself.

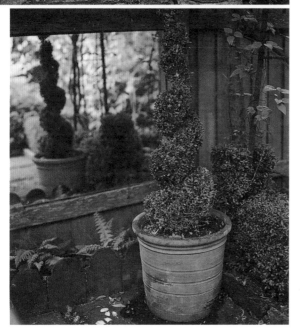

into the garden proper, you have to step through a wooden arch—an age-old motif that makes you pause and become aware of entering a special place. Ahead is a path laid in a pattern of cobblestones and brick that tapers slightly to create an illusion of greater length, and at its end is a yellow door that leads nowhere at all. Grown over with white roses and shrouded in mystery, the yellow door seems like another entrance to a further secret garden beyond.

This garden is made for wandering—and wondering. For such a small space, it has a remarkable array of places to sit and think and watch the wind in the trees. The magic is that each is distinct and entire in itself. Through clever but

Above left: Looking back to the house along the path that links the different areas of the garden. An earthenware pot stands among ferns to one side.

Left: The mirrors in the walls reflect the planting, including this topiary spiral, one of the many plants that have been clipped or trained into decorative shapes.

Above: Yellow folding chairs and a curly metal bench painted powder blue have been pulled up around a table made from an old sewing machine base. Mirrors set in the surrounding fences reflect the foliage and pleasantly confuse one's sense of space, while grapevines, kiwi plants, and clematis provide shade overhead. Sprays of *Buddleia alternifolia* are stunning in early summer.

"I believe profoundly in a beneficent spirit that lurks in gardens, turning tragedies into celebrations."

unobtrusive use of space and planting, Mirabel has created a series of sitting places for different times of day. The paved courtyard outside the kitchen has a Mediterranean air—the perfect place to enjoy a morning cup of coffee to the accompaniment of a tiny wall fountain. There's a dining area set up under a canopy of grapevines, kiwi, and clematis, where mirrors mounted in the side fences reflect the festivities ad infinitum. For privacy, a painted summerhouse stands on one side of the path—a peephole in the wall lets Mirabel see who is coming up the path. And a simple wooden bench, half hidden among the roses, ferns, and hellebores, has been positioned to enjoy the last evening rays of the sun at the end of the day.

Imaginative planting adds to the garden's magic. A recent convert to topiary, Mirabel clips and trains and twists her trees into startling shapes. A row of young eucalyptus trees was made into goblets, a pair of Kilmarnock willows have become felty gray mushrooms, and junipers trussed with climbing white roses are as close as Britain comes to Italian cypresses. While the evergreens are clipped into mad sculptures, the roses and climbers are allowed to roam, creating shady awnings and floral curtains that cast filigree shadows and screen the various sitting areas. Key to this garden's secrets is that you can never see it all at once—this gives an average-sized garden all the mystery and intrigue of much larger and grander creations. Only from a top-floor

Mirabel groups containers around the garden with casual flair.

Far left: Terra cotta pots and a sea kale forcer inhabit a shady corner, surrounded by ferns and hostas.

Left: Mirabel's son-in-law made these canopied shelves from a rough sketch. Beneath the little roof are displayed a green urn from Périgord, small glazed pots, and a variety of objects unearthed in the garden.

Right: Pleached linden trees join hands along one side of the garden. Panels of mirror are set into the fence, while blue-painted trellis gives added height.

Below: Another shelf, fashioned from a slab of scrap slate and cheap painted brackets, holds pale clay pots and scalloped roof finials from Greece. The colors look wonderful against the yellow brick wall.

window is the whole plan revealed—but that would threaten to break the spell. Come back after a year and the garden will have changed—trees will have moved or changed shape like a neverending game of grandmother's footsteps. It's all part of the magic, says Mirabel. "If an idea doesn't work, it leaves space for another to come along. I believe profoundly in a beneficent spirit that lurks in gardens, turning tragedies into celebrations." The best way to have a magical garden may be to believe in magic yourself.

sensual minimalism

Minimalism might be fashionable, but it need not exclude the sensual pleasures of life. That's the message of this modern roof terrace—a stylish exercise in wood, water, and stone.

Opposite and above left: Windows and doors open onto the deck to create a perfect indoor–outdoor space. Entertaining can flow effortlessly in and out, with elegant summer seating by B&B Italia around a low table. The spiraling branches of the corkscrew willow tree (right of main picture) are a wild, naturalistic contrast to the pared-down architecture.

Left: Silver birch trees look wonderful on a rooftop—like a tiny patch of woodland in the sky—and still allow a suggestion of the view through their small spring leaves. The fall foliage is bright yellow.

Above center: A series of screens around the terrace shield the living areas from the wind. Ready-cut red cedar was chosen for the deck, laid in different directions for greater impact. The roof had to be resealed in asphalt before the wood was laid on slats 12in (30cm) above it. A thick layer of Scottish beach pebbles brought up the levels, and the deck appears to hover just above it.

Above right: Stone is a good foil for the plants, such as these hostas, whose young spring growth is just pushing through. It also means minimal weeding.

Simple, pared-down modernity was what Fiona Naylor and her husband wanted when they moved to a penthouse loft in east London, but they didn't want anything too hard-edged. An architect, Fiona had no trouble creating an interior with comfortable yet minimalist style. The next task was to continue the look out of the floor-to-ceiling windows to the terrace, which wraps itself around the apartment's upper floor. Hard materials were limited to just wood and stone: red cedar for the decks and pathways, and grayish Scottish river pebbles for the rest. The combination of warm wood and pale pebbles creates a restful backdrop for the plants, many of which double as barriers against the wind. Like most roof terraces, this one is subject to quite harsh winds, which interfere with outdoor living, and limit the number of plants that will grow. Clever planting around the periphery of the garden converts the gusts into soothing rustling sounds that screen the traffic noise as well. Bold blocks of a few different species are used in particular areas—swishing bamboo and eucalyptus clipped into hedges on the south side, and on the north, around the dining area, ornamental grasses, elaeagnus, and slender birch trees. While creating the wind screens, great care was taken not to shut out the views—of an exhilarating cityscape that sparkles at night and shimmers in summer's haze.

Against a modernist backdrop such as this, architectural plants in bold containers might have created too hard and masculine a feel. But wilder-looking plants can provide the perfect contrast to modern architecture—think of how the tracery of the branches of a single silver birch transforms a boring office building. Fiona selected

Sprawling city views are one of the great features of the roof terrace, and though some screening against the wind was vital, it would have been a shame to shut them out. With expert advice from garden designer Lindsey Whitelaw of Whitelaw Turkington, plants were chosen for their ability to act as windbreaks as well as their good looks. Glossy-leaved *Elaeagnus x ebbingei* has been pruned into a hedge all along one side, while blocks of bamboo and eucalyptus were used elsewhere. Bamboos planted near the house (**right**) are valued for the swishing noise they make in the slightest breeze.

trees, shrubs, and grasses with a naturalistic growth habit to soften all the straight lines and create some subtle seasonal drama. A large twisted willow tree was a great choice—its bare winter branches are like strange spiraling sculptures till spring, when fresh lime-green leaves sprout forth. Ferns and hostas look good placed in groups against the natural-colored stone, while these Scottish river pebbles also act as a moisture-retaining and weed-suppressing mulch. Larger stones arranged in casual piles and circles here and there read like pieces of impromptu sculpture.

One of the advantages of urban roof terraces over gardens is that they get such good light. The simple structure and materials used here do not detract from the subtle effects of the changing light throughout the day and year, with the morning sun throwing dappled shadows on stone and wood, and the sunsets washing it all in a pinkish cast. Another of the simple sensual pleasures of this garden is water. Just a

One of the simple sensual pleasures of this garden is water. Just a shallow rectangle lined in galvanized metal is enough to create a welcome sense of stillness and calm, and reflect the leaves and sky.

shallow rectangle lined in galvanized metal is enough to create a welcome sense of stillness and calm, and reflect the leaves and sky. It is also safe for the couple's young children, who can use it for wading or sailing toy boats.

For this is a family garden, made for playing, relaxing, and entertaining. Alongside all the chic designer furniture and fashionable details, it is a place for having fun—the children have their sandbox screened off in a far corner, while the adults love to relax on the deck or chat in the evening sun over dinner with friends. Happily, the fact that this style of gardening is also very low maintenance leaves them even more time in which to do so.

Above left: Brass letters spell the plant name HOSTA across the cedar planks—decorative features are rare in a minimalist garden such as this, and their impact is all the greater for it.

Main picture and below left: This pool may be small and shallow, but it is one of the defining features of the roof terrace. The presence of water is immediately calming and cooling, and the reflections and tiny ripples on the surface of the water help to animate the space. In a clever detail, the galvanized metal trough appears to continue right under the raised deck.

naturally dynamic

Modern garden style needn't always mean straight lines and right angles. Taking inspiration from contemporary land art, a creative designer transforms a suburban garden with a sweeping curved wall.

When we think of modern gardens, we often think of straight lines. But curves can be just as contemporary as straights. Inspiration can be found in the fluid asymmetry of nature, which is the basis for the flowing forms of Japanese gravel gardens, or from abstract and environmental art. It's best to keep the idea simple and stick to one bold form—a circle, spiral, or serpentine curve—because too many elements will weaken the impact and make the space appear confused.

The land art of sculptor Andy Goldsworthy was the starting point for the sweeping S-shaped wall that has turned this sleepy garden in suburban London into an exciting, dynamic space. Thousands of slivers of gray slate create a low dry-laid stone wall that swoops and swirls its way around the garden, starting from the terrace behind the house to snake around the trunk of a tree and encircle a round wooden deck before sinking into a flowerbed at the back. In casting this single graphic figure on the ground

A sinuous slate wall snakes right through this suburban garden, turning it into an abstract picture that is particularly effective seen from an upstairs window. The pink flowering cherry tree, frowned on by fashion-conscious gardeners, has become a stunning central feature.

Once every year, Nature adds to the display with an art show of her own. The ornamental cherry comes into pink fluffy bloom in May and drops her petals over the garden like a pale confetti carpet.

in one grand gesture, the Brazilian designer Roberto Silva has pulled all the different areas in the garden together and created a unique layout that looks particularly stunning when viewed from above. The sweeping curve defines the area of lawn near the house, dividing it from the stone terrace beneath the tree and the wooden deck beyond. From an upstairs window it looks like a bold, bright abstract painting.

But the wall isn't only about aesthetics; it also supplies the focus for a much-used family garden. Just two feet (sixty centimeters) at its highest, it is safe for children to run

along, or for people to use as a bench or lounger to lie on in the sun. It makes a jump for lively dogs and a slalom for model cars. Plates can be balanced on it for a quick picnic lunch, or for summer parties, jars of candles can be lined up along its length. A pathway of compaction gravel follows the wall to the deck, a circular space often used as a stage for live music—outlets for electric guitars and amplifiers are hidden behind a large boulder jutting into the floor.

For cool contemplation, a water fountain has been incorporated into the stone cairns that stand like sculptures beneath the tree.

The use of natural stone runs like a theme throughout the garden, from the dry-laid stone wall made from slivers of gray slate right down to the smaller, more decorative features.

Far left and left: The large boulders emerging from the lawn and the deck behind it recall the rocks in Japanese gardens. Small boulders are piled into cairns.

Below left: Water trickles down the tallest stack of stones, pumped from an unseen reservoir, while pebbles of various sizes are scattered around the base of the cairns.

Below right: Larger flat stones are used as random stepping stones among the gravel under the tree.

Natural stone in different forms runs through this garden like a theme, from the slate wall itself right down to the boulder fountain and pebble mulch. All other elements in the garden have been kept purposefully simple, to support rather than detract from the impact of the curve. Furniture is minimal, while plants are mainly gray and green—lots of eucalyptus, umbrella-like tree ferns, and tufty stipa grasses. Japanese maples have been added for fall color, and for their reference to the Japanese gardens, which certain aspects of this garden recall. Like the boulders in gravel gardens signifying mountains, the large rock that rises out of the lawn serves as a symbolic reminder of the raw material behind all this artifice. There are no strong colors—no jarring tones. This is just as well, for once every year, Nature adds to the display with an art show of her own. The ornamental cherry—an unfashionable tree that has become the bane of the British suburbs—comes into pink fluffy bloom in May and drops her petals over the garden like a pale confetti carpet. For just a few short weeks, the effect is akin to that of an art gallery installation.

Below left: For a shock of color, the young lime-green leaves of crocosmias give way to flame-orange flowers in late summer.

Below right: For just a few weeks every May, the cherry-tree blossoms are scattered around the garden like pale pink confetti.

Above and below center: Planting is mainly confined to foliage plants to maximize the impact of the curved wall. Tufts of the gray-blue grass *Festuca glauca* emerge from a mulch of pebbles.

Main picture: The dry-laid wall was made from Welsh slate using a technique that uses no mortar. Though stunning to look at, its appeal is by no means just aesthetic. Two feet (sixty centimeters) at its highest point, it is just the right height for sitting on or lying in the sunshine, and its swooping, winding progress provides the focus for children's games. It can even be used as an impromptu picnic table, or have candles in glass jars or lanterns arranged along it after dark for a party.

part two

choosing the elements

furniture **54**

lighting **66**

art and sculpture **76**

containers **88**

decorative plant supports **100**

topiary **106**

summerhouses and retreats **112**

water features **118**

groundworks **124**

furniture

Furnish your outside space with pieces in keeping with your garden's style—from sleek modern loungers to retro chic to commissions from local craftspeople. Give garden antiques and thrift-store finds stylish linen cushions or an unexpected coat of paint.

Below: Modern furniture doesn't have to mean sacrificing comfort to style. These simple plastic bucket chairs by Robin Day are not only chic, they are also comfortable. The strong graphic shapes are shown to good advantage against an evergreen hedge. Like all the other furniture on this roof terrace (**opposite above and below left**), they combine elegance with ease of use.

It goes without saying that decorated gardens need furniture. If your garden is to become an outdoor room for living in, it will need somewhere to sit at the very least, and most likely a table and chairs for alfresco dining. People who especially enjoy life out-of-doors might even include a fireplace, or somewhere to sleep out on warm nights.

The most useful type of furniture, and that to consider before anything else, is seating. A garden with nowhere to sit is never going to be a relaxing place—and no matter how green and lush your lawn, you may want to do more than lie or sprawl. In large gardens there will be many different options for sitting areas—places to enjoy the morning sun with a cup of coffee, a sheltered overhang or awning providing shade from the midday sun, or a sundeck or terrace positioned to catch the last rays at the end of the day. There may be secret, secluded areas that call out for a single seat for solitary contemplation, or a romantic rose bower for a loveseat made for two. Or there may be sociable spaces where larger groups of people can sit, eat, or party. You may even end up creating some of these spaces from scratch, with sitting or socializing there in mind. In smaller gardens, however, you will probably have to choose between these options, or go for clever furniture that can serve several purposes.

One of the most interesting forms of garden furniture is seating that is built into the structure of the garden. At its simplest, this can just mean using the tops of low retaining walls of flowerbeds, steps, or terracing as extra seating. These features have a function in the garden anyway, but can accommodate visitors easily without the need for extra chairs. At the other end of the scale, more complex seating systems with permanent tables and other structures can be an integral part of the layout. Built-in seating needs careful thought and planning, of course, and it's

Furniture in one style and color suits a pared-down modern garden.
Contemporary pieces in white are casually grouped on this roof terrace,
including a Harry Bertoia basketweave chair from the Fifties and Robin
Day chairs (**above right**), and a sinuous lounger and table (**above and top**)
with coordinating leather-trimmed armchairs by B&B Italia.

Right: This folding slatted wooden chair has the simple graphic appeal
of abstract sculpture, silhouetted against the grass.

Main picture: In this stunning California garden by designer Judy Kameon, curly Fifties-style metal chairs are grouped around a glass-topped table near the swimming pool. The purple and chartreuse color scheme looks great against the pink-stained concrete walls. The cafe-culture look is in keeping with the sociable atmosphere that pervades the entire garden.

In large gardens there will be places to enjoy the morning sun or a deck or terrace positioned to catch the last rays at the end of the day.

most easily incorporated when building a brand-new garden. Its advantages are its permanence, and the way, if well designed, it can make a small space seem bigger and less cluttered. The furniture remains part of the garden, come rain or shine—and if you want to make changes or render hard surfaces more comfortable, you can always bring out bright cushions or coverings. Its major disadvantage is that it's often expensive, and you can't move it where you need it. So if you're planning permanent furniture, make sure you put it in the right place.

Most of us end up settling for at least some freestanding outdoor furniture, probably a table and chairs or a garden bench. These days, there's absolutely no excuse for going to the garden center and stocking up on slatted teak or white plastic—there are far too many other more interesting options around. The choice of old or new, antique or junk, designer classic or flat-pack will depend on your budget and taste and the style of your garden. Think carefully about the practicalities, as well as the look you want to achieve. If your furniture is to remain outside all year, it will have to withstand

This same garden has a variety of places to sit at different times of the day.

Above center: A table on the terrace beneath an enormous pepper tree provides a pleasantly shaded spot for lunch, with vintage Fifties metal chairs in cobalt blue and bright green pulled up around it. A paper lampshade, complete with a low-voltage bulb that lights up at night, hangs from the branches.

Above right: The pair of sun loungers with padded cushions are great for relaxing by the poolside, and can be trundled around on wheels to follow the sun.

Above left: Small mosaic-topped tables in a similarly curvaceous style pull up to hold a book or a drink.

the worst that the weather can throw at it, and this is where slate-topped tables and treated wooden benches come in handy. Or perhaps you like a bit of moss on your wooden table, or a touch of rust on your painted metal chairs, choosing to see such developments as desirable patinas rather than evidence of decay. If you don't mind shifting your furniture in and out of the shed or some other shelter, there are even more choices, but folding or stacking designs may prove the most convenient. There are many smart sets of tables and chairs available on the market. But don't think everything *has* to match. To me, there is something very attractive about a motley collection of old painted seats and slatted folding chairs grouped around a lunch table. The odd chintz armchair under a tree can also look charmingly eccentric.

For a modern deck or terrace, clean contemporary designs will probably be the answer, particularly if you have gone for that style inside. Look for twentieth- or twenty-first-century classics from modern designers (some of which can be found in secondhand stores and at garage sales as well as from specialized dealers). Off-the-rack styles from garden centers and department stores may well be cheaper and just as attractive. Or why not commission a one-of-a-kind piece from an up-and-coming designer? Contemporary designs can be customized—engraved with a fragment of poetry or carved with a pair of initials (such an object would make a perfect wedding or anniversary present).

Many people like the romantic look associated with antique garden furniture—and it associates surprisingly well with modern design. If you buy secondhand, you may have

Removable fabric cushions bring color as well as comfort to permanent outdoor furniture. In warmer climates they can stay out for much of the year, but are easy to bring inside during cold or wet weather.

Above left: The mauve and green of this daybed look good against the colors of the house, and make a stunning contrast with the roses and poppies in the foreground. Its low, wide shape accommodates two or three people, but is also perfect for one.

Above center: This metal-frame chair with rope seat is by Plain Air, a series of pieces designed by Judy Kameon based on classic designs from the Fifties.

Above right: Soft green cushions make this metal-framed sofa more comfortable and pick up some of the subtle foliage colors. Upholstery like this can be changed fairly easily from time to time to give the garden a different look. A chunk of hewn tree trunk makes a simple table at one end.

Seats can provide a touch of magic in a garden. A swing in a tree suggests lazy summer days. A bench beneath a rose arbor seems made for romance. And a seat half-hidden by overgrown plants is the perfect invitation to lose yourself in a book all afternoon.

For a modern deck or terrace, clean contemporary designs will probably be the answer, particularly if you have gone for that style inside. Look for twentieth—or twenty-first-century classics from modern designers.

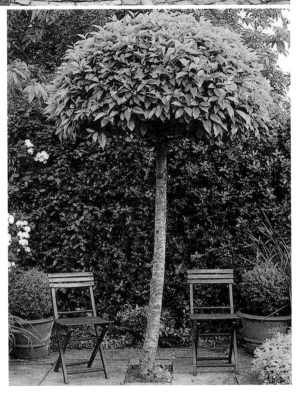

to decide whether to try to restore a piece to its original state, keep it as it is, or give it a new lease on life. Look out for attractive old benches with storage under the seats, graceful cast-iron benches, and round metal tables with curlicue legs. Some old designs can be given a modern twist with a coat of unexpected color or contemporary textiles. The garden designer Anthony Noel gives his tiny London

Traditional-style seating need not be dull. Chairs and benches can be jazzed up with a coat of bright paint or left to develop a natural distressed patina.

Above left: A Georgian-style metal bench is a suitably elegant choice for a walled town garden, flanked by linden trees and lavender bushes.

Above: Slatted wooden armchairs and a round table have been painted the same shade of green to match—a potted plant on the table helps to create an inviting and sociable space.

Right: The close-clipped tree canopy acts as a parasol for this pair of folding slatted chairs, painted an attractive blue.

Above left: Peeling paint is the perfect complement for wild naturalistic planting in a magical country garden.

Above: A beautiful shade of powder blue has given this curly metal bench a contemporary twist—the table is made from an old sewing machine base.

Left: Bluish purple is a good color for use among most shades of foliage. Here a period bench has been painted to highlight its intricate tracery, which shows up well against a dark evergreen backdrop. This is an excellent example of how the right seat can be used to terminate a view, or create a formal tableau alongside topiary and other features.

garden a new look every summer by painting all his furniture—thrift-store finds and antiques alike—turquoise or malachite green or shocking pink with black zigzags. The paint color can tie in with flowers and foliage and other garden features.

To be original, why not try making your own garden furniture? If you are handy with a saw, or know someone who is, there are books with instructions for seats in arbors, or circular benches to surround trees. But sometimes the best ideas are the simplest. I've seen great chunks of wood used as stylish stools, or a table made from a large antique tray on an upended pot. My own garden table was nailed-together wood from an old pallet, painted white.

Careful placing of furniture can help reinforce design features. A pair of chairs can flank an entrance, for instance, or a special bench provide the focus at the end of a path. A seat in the farthest reaches of the garden can provide the motive for a journey, especially if it takes in a good view. In the right place, and in the right light, a well-designed chair or bench can even read as sculpture. Seats can also provide a touch of magic in a garden. A swing in a tree suggests lazy summer days and the carefree joys of childhood. A bench beneath a rose arbor seems made for romance. And a seat half-hidden by overgrown plants is the perfect invitation to lose yourself in a book all afternoon.

Main picture: This simple wooden bench in Fovant Hut Garden in southern England is a beautiful fusion of sculpture with seating. Commissioned from local sculptor Mary Rawlinson, the English oak has been left unadorned save for the initials of the owners carved on the seat backs. The right seat in the right spot can enhance a corner of the garden and imbue it with special meaning, and a seat such as this would be an original way to mark a wedding or anniversary.

Top left: Wooden furniture can be left untreated for a natural look.

Top right: A fitting shade of green can look great in a garden—this verdigris bench is perfect.

Top center and above: Florist Sarah Raven, whose cutting garden is an exuberant exercise in bold and brilliant planting, doesn't stop at bright flowers, but chooses scarlet for a traditional planter's chair and shocking pink for a settle.

lighting

Creative lighting can transform your garden into a magical space for outside entertaining, from tree lights and candles to electric systems that cast dramatic shadows.

Lighting effects need not be complicated or expensive to transform your garden into a magical space for alfresco dinners or parties.

Above and above right: Improvised effects using strings of white tree lights among the foliage and sawn-off glass bottles containing votive candles supported on a spiral of wire. The salvaged aesthetic of the empty bottles works well in this small city garden.

Right and far right: Tree lights come on at dusk in the Los Angeles garden of Laura Cooper and Nick Taggart, glowing among grapevines and roses, and catching the glass beads that dangle from branches.

Lighting is not only vital for extending the life of your outdoor room late into the night, it is also useful for safety and security reasons. You want enough light to see and eat by, and to outline potential hazards such as steps or water in the garden. Beyond that, the function of outdoor lighting is to provide atmosphere—and lots of it. Too often, the only lighting in a garden is a security-style lamp on the rear house wall, which throws a prisonlike glare on the garden. Forget about this type of lighting, or keep it for security purposes only.

The main choice is whether to install an electronic system or rely on impromptu effects using candles and so on. Candles are the cheapest and easiest way of lighting the garden, and can also create the most magical effects. Glass or cut metal around the flame protects against wind as well as fire, and there are many attractive lanterns available in all shapes and sizes. Even plain votives in empty glass jars look lovely dotted around the garden—use small tumblers or Moroccan tea glasses to look pretty on tables. I collect tin lanterns from travels around the world, and suspend them from the branches of trees or line them in rows along the top of walls. For parties, flares on bamboo poles create a dramatic welcome, especially in winter—or follow the Italian example and set rows of large containerized candles on each side of steps and paths.

If you opt for electric lighting for your outside space, a professionally designed system is advisable, in large gardens at least. Though likely to be expensive, it is easily controlled by the flick of a switch, and if well installed should be safe and worry free. Larger, more elaborate systems should have special outdoor sockets and plastic-coated cable buried at least 18in (45cm) beneath the soil.

Main picture and above left: White lights and crystal flowers strung among the climbers on a simple wooden arbor create a magical atmosphere as the sun sets on this garden in the hills above Los Angeles. The table and chairs beneath are the perfect place to eat and drink with friends as the lights come on in the city below.

Above center and right: Back in London, the author's tiny courtyard is transformed into an intimate dining space after dark, with tin lanterns on tables and hanging in the trees. A curtain made from white tree lights hangs against the door, while other lights twinkle among the foliage and are reflected in a large mirror on the rear wall.

Placed high in a tree, a downlighter can look like the full moon shining through the branches and make filigree shadows on the ground. Uplighters work in the opposite way, buried at the base of plants to throw them into silhouette and cast dramatic shadows.

The somewhat stark design of this gravel garden benefits from dramatic lighting, designed by Sally Storey, at night. A circuit system has been professionally installed to highlight various features.

Left and above: Japanese-style boulders are lit by spotlights along the path's edge, casting shadows on the pale gravel.

Above center: Uplighters on the corners of a planter throw the topiary cone into sharp relief against the brick wall.

Above right: Concealed lighting bathes a pebble cairn in a golden glow. Uplighters placed close to climbers along a boundary project spectacular shadows up the walls or create subtle pools of light among the foliage. A sophisticated system such as this can be manipulated to create a variety of different effects according to the demands of the occasion.

A master switch in the house can control different circuits for different parts of the garden, and the effects can be monitored by remote control. A professional lighting expert should be employed to install this sort of outdoor lighting. For smaller gardens, low-voltage lighting with smaller fixtures, shorter cable runs, and a transformer to lower the voltage, is increasing in popularity. Such systems, which often include lamps on spikes that can be sunk into the soil where required, can be installed by an amateur—but make sure the wires are concealed in an area where spades and forks won't penetrate.

Different types of electric lighting can be focused on different areas in the garden. Downlighters can highlight features such as trees and sculpture from above, and create soft pools of light on a dining table. If placed high in a tree, a downlighter can look like the full moon shining through the branches and make filigree shadows on the ground. Uplighters work in the opposite way, buried at the base of plants to throw them into silhouette and cast dramatic shadows up and around the walls. They can be recessed behind glass around the edges of decks or paving, or hidden beneath the treads of stairs. Outdoor tree lights look magical studded like stars among the branches of a tree or wound around the posts of an arbor—the effect will be strongest if you stick to plain white bulbs. In my own garden I strung tree lights in strands from the back of the house to the rear garden wall to create the effect of bare rafters in a "ceiling." It looked a little like a Greek taverna to begin with, but the scented and flowering climbers soon entwined among the wires and softened the effect.

For entrances, electric lights on posts can make a formal approach set low along a driveway, while wall-mounted lights may be useful outside front doors—solar-powered fixtures that soak up natural light and come on after sunset are also available for these purposes. All garden lights must be waterproof—so if you can't find what you want at the garden center or hardware store, try bathroom suppliers or marine specialists for something more unusual. For a thoroughly modern effect, experiment with fiber optics, which send light through strands of glass fiber to create tiny individual points of light, or try projecting still or moving images around the walls. Neon light can look stunning in gardens—just a single line of electric blue or green will give a wall or deck a surreal modern edge, while a word or simple image mounted on a wall can look like contemporary sculpture.

Water features look especially good when lit at night. If you can, incorporate lighting when you are installing a pool or fountain. A soft gleam from the base of a pond or stream can bathe the whole garden in an otherworldly glow, and even cast shadows of fish swimming around the walls. The still surface of a small pond can also look lovely aglow with a flotilla of floating candles—choose citronella-scented ones and you should also keep mosquitoes at bay.

Soft, flickering candlelight is certainly the most decorative form of lighting for a garden. But do take care. Remember that glass and metal lanterns can get dangerously hot with even just a votive candle inside, and never leave a naked flame unattended. If you're tempted by some outlandish scheme for a party, take warning from this tale of an eccentric English *grande dame* who lived in Tangiers. Her spectacular summer parties were always the talk of

This contemporary roof terrace and glass conservatory was designed by Stephen Woodhams using uncompromisingly modern materials—glass, galvanized industrial grills, and corrugated metal. A sophisticated lighting system was integrated into the design to make the most of the shiny surfaces and the giant mirrors set into the sides of the solarium. A dazzling range of effects, including bright blue neon strips beneath the floor and state-of-the-art halogen lamps suspended on steel wires, can be controlled via a panel of dimmer switches. Lights around the door will even turn the glass from clear to opaque for extra privacy, cutting out the need for curtains or blinds. The overall effect is about as modern and urban as gardening gets. Strong architectural foliage is the only choice for such a space, and bamboos, spiky cordylines, and standard bay trees have been planted in simple galvanized pots and given a mulch of beach pebbles to match those in the fountain (shown on page 120).

Neon light can look stunning in gardens—just a single line of electric blue or green will give a wall or deck a surreal modern edge.

the town. One year, she decided to amaze her guests by sending into the crowds, at sundown, hundreds of tortoises with lighted candles stuck to their shells. She envisaged them wandering among the guests and illuminating the paths in a picturesque fashion. But, of course, the tortoises did nothing of the sort. Instead of sticking to the paths, they headed straight for the sanctuary of the long grass, bleached tinder dry by the Mediterranean sun. The garden went up in a wall of flames, and the guests had to rush home before their finery got singed.

Modern and exotic lighting features can be mixed within the same garden, creating a variety of effects and enhancing the planting.

Top: An old tin lantern with panes of stained glass from the souks of Morocco looks as decorative in the daytime as it does lit up at night.

Above: Lighting and water combine to make this small fountain in a ceramic bowl into an eye-catching feature.

Subtle lighting can enhance foliage effects and cast fascinating shadows among the plants.

Right: A length of tiny pinprick bulbs that came free with a magazine has been strung among the purple-leaved violets in this planter.

Below: Little lanterns on sticks rise from a group of variegated ferns, lamiums, and ivy in a shady corner of this London garden. They can be moved around the beds easily or poked into containers or pots—frosted glass gives a softer glow than clear.

art and sculpture

There's more to outdoor sculpture than concrete cherubs. Choose abstract pieces in natural materials, commission work for a particular site, or make your own land art from fallen wood or beachcombing finds.

Well-sited art and sculpture can make a purely pretty garden into a magical place. Larger pieces in stone, carved wood, or bronze seem to "inhabit" their surroundings and bring them to life. Even a fragment of stone engraved with a word or line of poetry can make a shady corner rich with meaning and association.

But you can have too much art in a garden. Pieces strewn about a large garden will turn it into a sculpture park or outside gallery, while smaller plots will look hopelessly cluttered. The impact of individual pieces will be lost in the profusion, so be strict. With larger sculptures at least, try to arrange things so only one piece is seen at once.

Part of the excitement of art and sculpture in a garden is happening upon it as you wander around. Site your art well, and a walk around the garden becomes a voyage of discovery. An unremarkable group of trees becomes a magic glade presided over by a stone figure or abstract obelisk, while a glimpse of sculpture at the end of a path or half-hidden by foliage invites exploration. For inspiration, you could visit sculpture gardens and parks, of which there are now many successful examples around the world, such as the artist Ian Hamilton Finlay's "Little Sparta" in Scotland, which is packed with classical references and witty stone inscriptions. Study the work of sculptors such as Isamu Noguchi and Barbara Hepworth, land artists like Andy Goldsworthy and Richard Long, and American landscape architect Martha Schwartz. When it comes to buying your own art, go for the best you can afford. And if the work of established sculptors is beyond your means, keep an eye on local galleries and art

The balcony terrace of this California garden designed by Isabelle Greene is an exercise in the careful placement of objects. Sensitively positioned on slatted wooden platforms, these ancient artifacts have been elevated to the ranks of sculpture. Part of the owner's ceramic art collection, one can imagine them getting lost in a more crowded corner of the garden, whereas here, against the uncluttered white walls, they come into their own. There is a Zenlike simplicity about the space—the bare concrete walls, uninterrupted save by a blood-red bougainvillea, and the simple vessels, rich in patina and texture, displayed on low Japanese-style tables.

school shows. Commissioning work for a particular place in the garden is even more fun than buying art—it is a true collaboration between the owner, the artist, and the site. Choose an artist who is sensitive to the place and will select forms and materials in keeping with the surroundings—some outdoor sculpture looks as if it has been parachuted down from outer space. The materials for site-specific work may be right under your nose in the form of old wood or salvaged stone. The British designer Ivan Hicks transformed a garden using only rocks and rusted metal found discarded on the site— he formed a spiral of white flints in a circle of moss, and made a magic woodland with metal springs and squares of mirror glass suspended from the trees. If a tree in your garden or neighborhood blows down in a storm, the wood could be given new life as a sculpture.

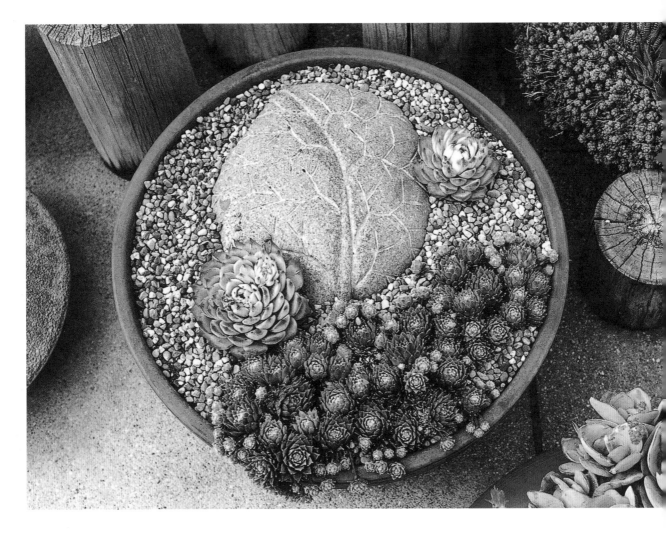

Stone is a natural choice to create a sculptural presence in the garden—and it need not be carved into traditional figurative pieces to look effective.

Above far left: A well-chosen boulder with attractive markings looks the part in this Japanese-style gravel garden—rocks in traditional Japanese gardens are a visual and symbolic reminder of mountains.

Below far left: This stunning slate urn by sculptor Joe Smith was made using dry-laid stone techniques.

Above left: Rocks piled into simple stone cairns have been incorporated into a sculptural fountain—a natural complement to the curved stone wall that snakes through this garden.

Above right: Succulents whose leaves form a geometric rosette are strong sculptural presences in themselves. They look good displayed here with a flat carved rock in a shallow bowl topped with a gravel mulch.

Or there may be other materials with relevance to your local area—be it urban or rural—that could take on new form.

The garden created by the late film director Derek Jarman in Dungeness on England's southern coast is one of the best examples of local salvage made anew—discarded lumber from the beach, bleached wood, pebbles, and fragments of rusty metal are reincarnated as modern-day menhirs, mad scrolling sculptures, and stone circles in the pebble beach. It has many imitators, but this style of garden only works when the objects have local or personal significance. If you live at the edge of a slate quarry, or in the heart of a busy city, you will probably create a very different garden full of very different objects.

Above: Salvaged treasures create an almost surreal tableau on the rear wall of this building in the gardens at Bryan's Ground.

Above right: Even objects that might end up in the trash can can be recycled as garden art. In this wonderful California garden, empty blue glass bottles look beautiful sprouting from the branches of a tree—an instant artwork that costs nothing. Glass bottles can also be plunged into the soil, neck up, to create an attractive edging for paths.

The art of illusion can be employed with spectacular effect in gardens.

Opposite left: At the late set designer Tony Duquette's home in Beverly Hills, the grand and exotic-looking sculptures are often makeshift concoctions of salvaged plastic and metal.

Opposite right: Mirrors play beguiling tricks on one's sense of space. This arched mirror frames what looks like the entrance to another world. Siting the mirror off the visitor's direct angle of vision and giving it a chunky mosaic and shell frame help keep up the illusion of a doorway—the spell is broken if you see your own face.

Some "found objects" are interesting enough in themselves without artistic intervention. Architectural fragments, unusually shaped tree stumps or driftwood, even intriguing pieces of rusted machinery can take on sculptural significance if a place can be found where they are seen to best advantage. This is the first step toward becoming your own artist. Even if you have no training, you can try your hand at land art with a single cairn of stones. The key is to keep things simple—if the shape and materials are interesting, the play of light and shadow should do the rest. Repeating the same object many times can imbue it with sudden

Site your art well, and a walk around the garden becomes a voyage of discovery. An unremarkable group of trees becomes a magic glade presided over by a stone figure or abstract obelisk, while a glimpse of sculpture at the end of a path invites exploration.

Above: A plaster Buddha, decorated with necklaces, from a shrine in India sits beneath a large bamboo, bringing an air of calm contemplation to a garden in a busy area of London.

artistic status: five empty vessels ranged along a wall, for instance, or a line of shiny galvanized plant supports casting shadows on a lawn. Even empty blue glass bottles pushed over the tops of posts or wires make something beautiful out of nothing. Try things out. Chop and change. You can experiment endlessly with this sort of impromptu, impermanent art.

Smaller, more decorative pieces can be great fun to make and are wonderful presents. Create a chandelier from favorite pebbles, sand-worn glass, and crystals strung on fishing line, or a wind chime from driftwood and old glass beads or rusty metal spoons. Or customize pots and plant supports to make them unique works of art.

Art doesn't just have to sit there looking beautiful—it can work for you as well. If you are pressed for space, or already possess a number of figurative or abstract pieces, why not think of functional objects as potential works of art? Commission a sculptor to custom design a bench or table, or have a piece of slate engraved with words or images so it can then be set on legs. Even traditional garden buildings such as summerhouses can be

Below: In Andy Cao's glass garden in Los Angeles, artworks have to compete with the bizarre materials and bold graphic planting it contains. A terra cotta pot on a metal stand has been placed among this "rice field" of feather grass and blue glass chips. The low retaining wall also twinkles with glass, while clear glass marbles glitter in the foreground.

Above left and above: Exotic statuary is one of the key features that gives Tony Duquette's Los Angeles garden its unique timeless atmosphere.

Right: Attractive glass bottles can be recycled as sculpture by slipping them over the ends of wood or wavy metal—a lot more fun than taking them to the bottle bank.

Sculpture doesn't have to be bought from galleries or commissioned from artists. With imagination and ingenuity, found objects that have some intrinsic interest can be transformed into focal points.

Right: Jan Howard made this wind chime by suspending flattened old spoons from fishing line.

Center: Garden designer Ivan Hicks is a magician with salvaged junk. He used only materials found on site to bring an air of mystery and intrigue to this garden. Long-buried bottles hung on wire from the branches add to the impact of a simple wind chime **(above)**, while a spiral of rusted metal rises like a serpent from the lawn **(below)**.

Far right: A collection of discarded hardware, attractively rusty, hangs from a hook against the backdrop of the garden. The impact of these old tools gathered in a suspended tableau is infinitely greater than if they had been displayed separately.

given a fresh artistic slant. Ben Wilson's woodland retreats and walkways that swoop out of the undergrowth high into the tree canopy are landscape art at its most exhilarating—why sit in a boring old shed when you could perch up with the birds, with talismanic carvings and wind chimes all around? And Richard Craven's treehouses look like arboreal sculptures, but also include a tray and pulley for hauling up snacks and bottles of wine. You can also commission smaller features such as sundials and birdbaths as working works of art.

Sculpture associates particularly well with water in gardens. William Pye is one of the masters in this field, using reflective surfaces to enhance the natural qualities of still and running water. Angela Conner creates kinetic water sculptures where the force of the moving water makes the entire piece move. The siting of almost any sculpture near water will increase its impact—a huge Ben Nicolson white marble relief is reflected in a lily pond at J. P. Getty's Sutton Place. And at Charles Jencks' Garden of Cosmology

The right object can transform a forgotten corner of the garden. A fragment of architectural salvage or a shape carved on site from a fallen tree can be just as effective as formal sculpture. Even the most unpromising objects can look effective if cleverly used.

Opposite left: A truncated classical column, wooly with moss and lichen, contributes to the mood of romantic abandon in Marc Schoellen's Luxembourg garden.

in Scotland, ambitious earthworks created crescent-shaped lakes and spiral promontories that became artworks in their own right. Even in the most minimal urban gardens, designers are experimenting with modern lighting—strips of electric-blue neon or projections of images onto white walls—to showstopping artistic effect.

Nature, of course, is the greatest artist of all. I sometimes look at the perfection of a single shell or flower and wonder why humans bother to try to compete. Leave spaces in your garden where the unassuming artistry of nature can be honored and admired. Take inspiration from the genius of James Turrell, who installs roofless modern shrines in landscapes for the observation of the changing sky and light, and leave a blank wall or a bare patch of grass where the seasons can work their own magic.

Opposite above right: A fallen tree was transformed into this large graphic pod shape in Peter Farrell's English garden—it is now sprouting vegetation of its own.

Above: Also in Peter Farrell's garden, architectural fragments such as this Ionic capital (**left**) and a stone sphere reminiscent of an old cannon ball (**right**) are used to punctuate the planting.

Opposite below: In a stroke of improvisatory genius, garden designer Christina Oates used five silvery spirals sold as tomato supports to bring a sculptural presence to Fovant Hut Garden in southern England. The strong graphic shapes, grouped in a line, look great against the backdrop of leyland cypresses clipped into columns. As a general rule, odd numbers have a more dynamic impact than even numbers in such arrangements.

containers

Containers are a fantastic way to create both instant and lasting style in your garden. A few attractive plants in well-chosen pots can transform the dullest, barest garden in the space of a few hours, while smaller treasures, placed at eye level or grouped around doors or windows, can give pleasure all year round.

Above and opposite: Plants of the same type can be grouped in the same container—they look good together and enjoy the same growing conditions. Succulent plants, which like dry, well-drained soil, are happy displayed in shallow pans and bowls with a mulch of small pebbles or gravel. On this balcony terrace in California, they can stay outside all year round, but in colder climates, some of the more tender varieties would need to be brought under cover for winter.

Center: Old buckets and trash cans have been pressed into use for plants in this front yard. The dull gleam of the metal associates well with silver-leaved plants such as lavender.

A plant in an attractive pot can make a new garden instantly feel like home. When our plot was still in the planning stage, I used containers to jazz up the white walls while I was waiting for climbers to grow. Taking inspiration from the courtyards of Córdoba in Spain, I strung galvanized buckets of bright red and pink geraniums up and down the trellis. The climbers are now established and the buckets remain, but the flowers are white. As you gather plants for a new garden, you can plant them in pots while you decide on their permanent positions. You can rearrange the groups to see what looks good with what, and experiment by moving certain pots around the beds. When the plants have found their places in the ground, the containers will be free for seasonal plantings of spring bulbs or bright summer annuals.

Pots of plants can create seasonal change and interest within a framework of more permanent evergreen plantings—whether the latter is in flowerbeds or more containers. This is a handy way to garden if you are too busy to do much maintenance—a few hours of activity at certain times of year will more than pay you back, and you can change the style and color scheme easily from year to year. Fall is the time to plant bulbs for the spring—stick to one type per pot, such as the beautiful blue *Iris reticulata* which will flower when little else is in bloom, shallow pans of multistemmed white hyacinths, or the more delicate daffodil species such as 'Old Pheasant's Eye' or 'Actaea.' Tulips,

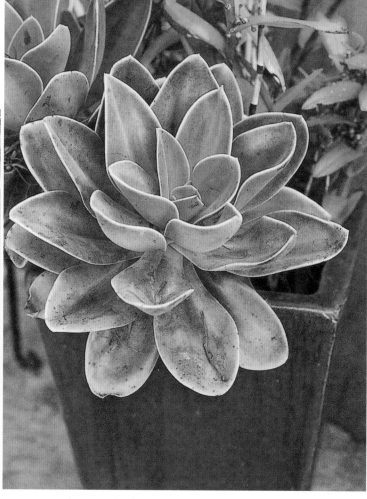

which somehow look happier in pots than serried like soldiers in a bed, can also be planted now—my favorites are the black-purple 'Queen of Night,' milky-green 'Spring Green,' and 'Prinses Irene,' which is orange with a dull purple flame. It's fun to watch the progress of bulbs, from the first pale nibs poking through the soil to the emergence of furled leaves and final opening of the buds. As each pot comes into bloom, it can be moved where it can be admired to best advantage—or even brought inside into a cool room. When the flowering period's over, the pots can be put away—there's none of the worry of how to hide the dying foliage in a bed. For summer, sow or plant annuals such as fragrant nicotianas, nasturtiums in every shade of orange, red, and yellow, or *Cerinthe major* 'Purpurascens' with its peacock-blue bracts and bright violet flowers. For

more permanent plantings, many architectural foliage plants, ornamental grasses, and different types of lavender are well suited to containers.

Matching the right plant to the right pot is one of the many pleasures of container gardening. There is a greater variety of tubs and planters on sale today than ever before, in all sorts of sizes, colors, and materials, from galvanized metal to painted wood to brightly glazed clay. And don't forget the joys of salvage—attractive and original containers can be made from old tin buckets, builders' troughs, cracked teapots, and empty olive oil cans—you name it, and you can probably make a pot out of it. The crucial thing is to make sure the containers are large enough—remember that smaller pots will require more watering—and that they have adequate drainage. Plants in pots without holes in

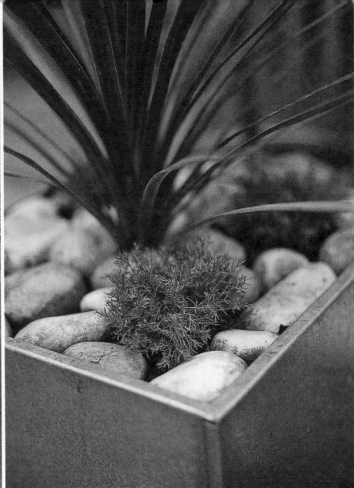

Clean graphic containers in bold colors and modern materials complement architectural plants.

This page: Tall terra cotta pots with a cobalt-blue glaze are the perfect foil for the geometric shapes and soft glaucous foliage of succulent plants—the pink leaves pick out the color of the wall behind.

Center above and below: Smaller pots create a bigger impact arranged in pairs or multiples. Metal, shiny or distressed, combines stylishly with gray- or silver-leaved plants.

Far right above and below: Zinc is a popular choice in modern gardens, particularly where metal has been used elsewhere. A mulch of pebbles and moss shows off the strappy leaves of this cordyline, which sits on a modern metal grill.

Above: Potted plants can be grouped on tables in the garden just as they would be inside the house. Cacti and succulents have unusual graphic shapes that are shown off to good advantage in a line of pots on this elegant glass-topped table.

Above right: Glass and ceramic chips have been worked into the concrete on this long low planter, filled with the leafy rosettes of crassulas and other succulents.

Top: Mosaic looks particularly good in gardens when it is confined to a few subtle colors. Containers covered in mosaic patterns can be bought from stores or commissioned from mosaic artists, but it is not hard to make your own, given a little practice. This tall pot has been covered with cobalt-blue tiles and fragments of blue and white pottery. It will look wonderful against the red strawberries when they start to fruit.

Right: Sempervivums, or hens-and-chicks, were traditionally planted on rooftops to ward off witches, but they look just as good in this glazed green pot. They have multiplied from just one or two tiny plants, and the little offsets have started to spill over the side of the pot.

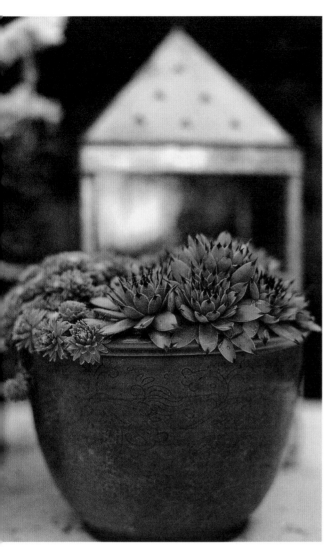

the bottom will become waterlogged and die, so check the base for holes and if necessary drill some more. Place a few pot shards or flat stones over the hole or holes, then a few inches of gravel to make sure the roots won't sit in water. Only then comes the soil, which should be chosen for the plant in question. In container gardening, every plant can be given its exact requirements—ericaceous medium for acid-lovers like azaleas and blueberries, and so on. When making more permanent plantings, it's a good idea to work some well-rotted manure or slow-release fertilizer such as fish emulsion or bone meal into the soil. The top few inches of soil can be renewed every other year until the plant may eventually need to be moved to a larger pot.

When your plants are installed, consider a mulch of gravel, small pebbles, or shells. Covering the soil surface not only looks attractive, it helps conserve moisture and keep down weeds, and may even deter ravaging slugs and snails. I've used purple aquarium gravel (from pet stores) on some of my pots, which continues to look good when the plants die down in winter. A friend collects empty oyster and scallop shells for his palms and bamboos.

Containers work well for today's nomadic generation, who may not stay put in one place long enough to establish permanent flowerbeds. Pots and containers can create a garden in as long as it takes to gather your pots and plants, but can also be taken with you when you move on. If you

Matching the right plant to the right pot is one of the many pleasures of container gardening. Don't forget the joys of salvage—attractive and original containers can be made from old tin buckets, builders' troughs, cracked teapots, and empty olive oil cans—you name it, and you can probably make a pot out of it.

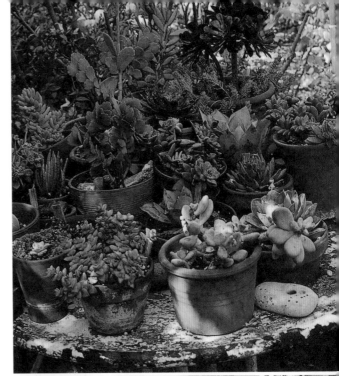

have a small city plot but big dreams of rural acres, plant young trees and shrubs in large trash cans—I have used a mixture of shiny galvanized ones bought from hardware stores, dull metal ones found discarded on the street when we switched to plastic wheeled bins, and old fluted metal laundry tubs from junk and antique stores. The trees will be fine for quite a few years—indeed, some specimens, such as fig trees, do well with their roots restrained. They can be liberated into open soil if and when you want to plant them in a permanent site.

The other exciting virtue of containers is their mobility within the garden. They can be moved around according to the plants' needs, or your own—some might require more sun or shade at different times of the year, while large tubs on wheels containing trees can be trundled about to give you shade in summer. But containers needn't be confined to trees, shrubs, and flowers. You can have a containerized herb garden or vegetable patch—I grow enough for salads all summer in a couple of old metal grape-treading vats from France. Or what about a container pond—a large ceramic bowl can make a lovely little pool for a single water lily or bubble fountain. One of the most unusual uses for a container was devised by some friends of mine. I found an old builders' trough on casters when we were renovating our house and was thinking of constructing a large wooden tub on top for a silver birch tree so I could move it around our yard. In the end I gave it to my friends, who made a mobile lawn for their dog. Their apartment building has a communal roof terrace with an asphalt floor that gets so hot

Succulent plants almost always look good grouped together in pots. Their complex geometric forms and subtle colors associate well together, and they share the same growing requirements. Well-drained soil and a sunny, frostfree spot are all they need to keep on growing and multiplying year by year.

Main picture: Echeverias have attractive red and yellow flowers.

Top: A rich variety of crassulas, aloes, sempervivums, and other succulents are clustered in weathered terra cotta pots on this rusty painted table—the glaucous gray-greens and pale mauves look good against the dark red of *Aeonium arboreum* 'Schwartzkopf' at the back.

Above: Spiky succulents, mulched with white chips in matching terra cotta pots, make a bold sculptural statement near an entrance gate. According to *feng shui* principles, spiky plants are effective at warding off intruders.

in summer that the dog cannot lie down. The new "potted lawn"—just a few square feet of sod rolled out onto a shallow bed of soil—is as popular with their neighbors as it is with Biscuit the dog. It is now much in demand for parties and barbecues elsewhere on the rooftop—provided that Biscuit will allow.

Main picture: A collection of old galvanized tubs, buckets, watering cans, and other containers in a corner of a garden in Holland. Some may be waiting to have holes drilled in their bases to become planters, but in the meantime they look attractive arranged on shelves against the foliage.

Above left: Large stones that look like giant goose eggs have been placed on the soil in the pot holding this little clipped tree.

Top center: Pots don't necessarily have to be filled with plants. This empty earthenware pot looks lovely against the green hedge and hills beyond in the formal rose terrace of this Scottish hillside garden.

Above center: Tall terra cotta "long Toms" are a good choice for topiary shapes. There is enough space for this boxwood ball to grow to a good size, and the depth of the pot means the soil shouldn't dry out too quickly.

Above right: Weathered ornamental terra cotta pots containing small trees are lined on a narrow strip of lawn in this Luxembourg garden. Citrus trees were traditionally grown in this type of pot in English country gardens and brought inside to shelter in ornate orangeries during the winter months.

Regardless of their function as containers for plants, terra cotta pots and other garden artifacts can be attractive features in themselves if they are displayed with an eye for their individual quirks and qualities.

Above left: This large earthenware pot has enough presence to act as the centerpiece for this ornamental potager that forms part of a California garden.

Top: Collections of similar objects are always appealing. Here, old watering cans, unremarkable, perhaps, on their own, create a pleasing picture grouped together on shelves.

Above: A perfect pink rose is shown off against the dull gray of this dented metal container. Take a bucket or small pot with you as you walk around the garden snipping blooms for the house. Or, if you have visitors, leave simple floral arrangements around the garden.

Main picture: Just outside the back door at Bryan's Ground, some old wooden shelves have become a cabinet of curiosities, with plants and other objects arranged in little tableaux in the various compartments. Playing on the idea of the traditional "Primrose Theater," in which potted specimens were displayed on shelves with a roof to keep the rain off their powdery leaves and painted faces, the plants are joined here by sheeps' skulls, seed heads, special pebbles, and other treasures.

You can have a containerized herb garden or vegetable patch. Or what about a container pond—a large ceramic bowl can make a lovely little pool for a single water lily or bubble fountain.

Main picture: A spreading tree canopy adds to the shade created by climbing roses and other plants trained up this large wooden arbor. Its chunky design means it would be strong enough to support even quite heavy plants. Structures such as this are like leafy tunnels, cool and soothing to walk under in the heat of summer, and are an attractive way of linking one area of the garden to another.

Center: Sometimes plants themselves create the support for others. Here, a beautiful flowering maple is scrambling through the branches of a citrus tree—the colors of flowers and fruit make a stunning combination against the pale blue wall.

Left: An impromptu arbor has been fashioned out of rusty reinforcing bars used in the construction of concrete-frame buildings. The twisted frame supports a golden hop and the star-like purple flowers of the vigorous climber, *Solanum crispum*.

decorative plant supports

Part of the fun of decorating a garden lies in making even extremely functional objects such as plant supports beautiful. Why go for boring old bamboo stakes when you can have a woven willow wigwam or pretty painted pickets for just a little extra time and effort?

Plant supports can be divided loosely into two groups: larger, more architectural features up which a variety of climbers can be grown, and smaller devices for training or staking more compact collections or individual plants. As with all other aspects of the garden, the style and materials used should reflect the overall look you have chosen, as well as their strength and suitability for the plants you wish to grow.

Arches are useful to frame an entrance to the garden, or mark the transition to another area within the design. Climbing roses, clematis, or honeysuckle scrambling around an arch will make a lovely fragrant bower in summer—plant different varieties on either side and they will intertwine overhead. Arbors are a series of arches, joined at intervals to make a sort of tunnel. When covered with plants in

Clean straight lines look best in a modern garden, while more rustic combinations of woven willow and twigs are great for a wilder cottage-garden border or vegetable patch.

summer, they provide welcome shade—in fact, the earliest examples were probably created so women could walk outside during the day avoiding the perils of suntans or freckles. Both arches and arbors can be bought in many different styles, or created quite cheaply and easily yourself. Whether built from chunky painted wood, reclaimed scrap lumber, or modern or aged metal, they can provide support for many different plants, among them grape- and kiwi vines as well as roses, morning glories, and other flowering climbers. Sometimes just one type of plant can look dramatic: one of the most frequently photographed arbors is that at the late Rosemary Verey's garden in western England—it drips with bright yellow laburnum flowers in May and early June, and is underplanted with purple alliums. But you don't have to confine yourself to purely decorative plants—many varieties of squash and cucumber can be trained over arches, and look lovely with trailing nasturtiums flowering in their midst. When it comes to smaller plant supports, you can be as simple or elaborate as you like.

Above left: The designer Jonathan Bell screened off his small city garden from his neighbor using chunky wooden trellis and ivy. The result affords privacy while still letting through some light and air.

Above right: A clematis has been planted at the base of this simple steel arbor in a garden designed by Sue Berger (see also previous page, right). Most climbers need initial training, but will soon scramble up the posts. Though clematis flowers follow the sun, their roots prefer to be in the shade or covered by a large stone.

Above: This rusty metal rose arch frames the view of the little corrugated garden shed beyond, and the overhead foliage also helps soften the architecture of the tall buildings that overlook the garden.

Right and opposite center: The plant supports in Sarah Raven's Cutting Garden in southern England are decorative features in their own right. This brightly painted teepee (**opposite**) provides a strong sculptural presence in the flowerbeds all year round, and the color makes a splendid contrast with the dark maroon sweet peas that have almost smothered another support nearby. The twiggy wigwam (**right**) is slightly more rustic in feel and looks wonderful rising from a mass of foliage. This, too, will provide support for sweet peas for Sarah's exuberant flower arrangements. Structures such as this can add welcome height to the garden, or serve to anchor the design at the center or corners of beds.

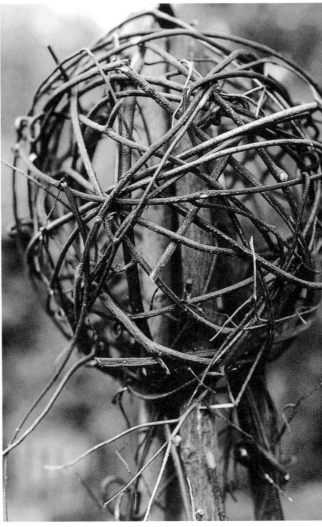

Left: Even the most unlikely materials—such as these old bed springs—can be colonized as supports by climbers. The coils of rusty wire look like suspended sculpture.

Above and right: Jan Howard's garden is a showcase for the plant supports she designs herself in wood and rusted metal. The simple wooden structure provides support for fragrant roses and honeysuckle, while the smaller metal stakes can be plunged into flowerbeds to prop up plants that have started to flop. Many of her designs are crowned with a ball—either solid metal or a tangle of woven wood.

Just painting your stakes in a single strong color can enhance their appearance and link the garden together—choose dark green or blue to merge with the foliage, or bright orange or purple to complement the flowers. Clean straight lines look best in a modern garden, while more rustic combinations of woven willow and twigs are great for a wilder cottage-garden flowerbed or vegetable patch. Wigwams and obelisks make great supports for fragrant sweet peas, and can be bought ready-made or in easy-to-assemble kits. Metal versions look stylish, but make sure the plants you are growing will not be harmed when they heat up in the sun. Or again, you can always make your own. Crown your wigwams with a decorative feature such as a wooden finial or ball of twigs, and cover sharp ends of stakes with shells or bottles or terra cotta staketops to avoid spiking yourself while weeding. Glass beads or other shiny objects can be strung on wires between the stakes to catch the light and ward off birds.

Decorative plant supports contribute a striking vertical element to the garden—positioned symmetrically or at the corners of beds, they can help anchor the overall design. And what's more, they will continue to look good long after the flowers have faded and the herbaceous plants and annuals died down. Features such as these inhabit a garden all winter long, and look wonderful in frost, or with a light covering of snow.

topiary

With careful trimming and training, the plants in your garden can grow into living sculptures. Fashion trees and bushes into simple cones, cubes, and spirals, or make a mobile topiary garden in containers.

Plants can form part of the decorative structure of your garden. A row of trees becomes a green corridor, where the tree trunks read as columns, while clipped hedges work as leafy screens or walls. Individual trees or bushes, planted in pots or in the ground, can also be trained and trimmed into a variety of stunning sculptural effects.

The species most commonly used for topiary are the dense-leaved evergreens boxwood (*Buxus*), yew (*Taxus baccata*), and bay (*Laurus nobilis*), but many other shrubs such as juniper, rosemary, lavender, camellias, and holly can be used with equally good results. Hawthorn is popular for its thick summer foliage, but its deciduous habit means the solid framework will be lost in winter—not great for mazes, but good for adding seasonal variety. Lawson cypress (*Chamaecyparis lawsoniana*) is quick to establish, but must be clipped frequently to keep it under control.

Topiary has a long history in traditional garden design, but can very easily be given a contemporary twist. Just a gently sloping top to a hedge, which may follow or complement a contour in the surrounding landscape, can give a subtly modern edge to a design. The flowing curved hedges in designer and nurseryman Piet Oudolf's own garden at Hummelo in the Netherlands make a stylish formal stage set, against which his new perennial plantings and wild wayward grasses are shown to good effect. Pleached lindens or hawthorns can be given a lower

Formal courtyard gardens look good with period architecture, and this front garden, designed by Sue Berger and Helen Phillips, is a good example of a modern approach to topiary. The geometry of the boxwood beds is softened by looser, naturalistic planting, with euphorbias and crocosmias adding splashes of lighter green. The young linden trees may later be pleached to surround the inner space.

At night, particularly under a full moon, topiary can look mysterious—even magical. You can almost imagine the plants moving around the garden with a life of their own.

"skirt" in a contrasting color or texture of foliage—a bit like painting a room in a different color up to the height of a chair rail. And the current fashion for "cloud topiary" can turn a plain boxwood or yew hedge into a mass of billowing bulges. The thing to avoid is anything resembling the whimsical teapots and peacocks of yesteryear. Today's topiary is graphic and streamlined: think spheres, cubes, and cones—at the very most, a simple spiral.

Individual plants clipped into shapes provide the best opportunities for artistic expression. You can buy plants ready trimmed, or wield the shears yourself, either trusting your own instincts or following instructions in a book. Let the shape and size of the plant dictate the finished form.

The Dutch garden of Manus Hijmans and Nellie Christiaans is an example of topiary at its best.

Above: The topiary table and chairs always raise a smile with visitors—note the potted plant on top.

Main picture and right: Contemporary gardeners stick to simple shapes for topiary, preferring cubes, cones, and tier shapes to complicated birds or cute teapots. Potted plants can be clustered in groups and moved around the garden. This doesn't rule out a little elegant humor, however.

Low rounded mounds are easy to begin with, and look surprisingly effective interspersed with freer-growing herbs and grasses. Strong vertical shapes such as obelisks and pyramids are useful for framing entrances or anchoring the design of potagers or parterres. And a line of lollipop standards is always stylish, either growing out of pots, or rising from leafy pedestals of clipped boxwood or yew. A variety of different shapes, positioned in informal groups, can populate a garden like guests at a cocktail party. At night, particularly under a full moon, topiary can look mysterious— even magical. You can almost imagine the plants moving around the garden with a life of their own.

Topiary works well in containers, and the current fashion for a group of single shapes in shiny pots works well on balconies and in small modern gardens. As topiary takes time to mature, these mobile plant sculptures can be taken with you if and when you move home. For a faster effect, wire frames can be made or purchased for training climbers into architectural shapes. Ivy works best for a year-round effect, but could be interspersed with clematis or a passionflower vine. The latter look lovely grown around a large openwork ball, so that individual blooms can be seen to good advantage. The balls could be mounted on poles and placed in open ground, where they would provide sculptural interest in winter when the flowering plants have died down.

Right: A formal style featuring clipped hedges and topiary hedges often works well in the immediate environs of the house. At Marc Schoellen's garden in Luxembourg, the heavily stylized shapes and low hedges around the flowerbeds near the entrance contrast with the larger-scale alleés and effects in the main garden beyond.

Above left: Lavender and rosemary are among the many plants that can be clipped into low mounds in the midst of more naturalistic planting—a good way to start off with topiary, and useful for keeping such plants neat and compact. Lavender should be pruned just after flowering, and never into the dead wood.

Above: Boxwood clipped into a cluster of small balls provides a striking contrast with the large, attractively indented leaves of the plume poppy, *Macleaya cordata*.

Below left: Boxwood plants clipped into spirals make an elegant entrance to this good-looking greenhouse.

Above left: This simple white summerhouse in the Farrell family's garden has open sides to frame different views of the garden. Structures such as this can fulfill a variety of functions within the garden. They not only provide pleasant, shady places to sit, but can also provide the focus for a vista, or screen compost piles or other more functional areas of the garden beyond.

Above: Farther up the garden path, Mirabel's wonderful "Cat House," designed by Richard Craven, has been positioned to afford a view across the garden. Beautifully decorated in mauve, blue, and orange, inside and out, it contains an antique settle with plenty of storage space beneath the seat. A peephole in a side wall allows Mirabel to see who is coming up the path.

summerhouses and retreats

There's nothing like a garden building to make you feel at home outside. They can range from elaborate outdoor rooms complete with comfortable furniture and cooking facilities to simple open structures providing little more than shelter from the sun, wind, and rain. Placed well, they can play an important part in the garden's overall design.

An attractive garden building can provide welcome height and color, the focus for a vista, and added interest in winter. In historic gardens, follies and temples were placed primarily for their aesthetic impact in the landscape; the shade and shelter they provided were often incidental. But today's garden buildings are functional as well as beautiful—places for eating and entertaining, outside offices, or playrooms or sleeping space for summer guests. They can also double as useful storage for garden furniture, lawnmowers, and other tools.

There are companies that specialize in supplying outdoor buildings to set designs or individual specifications. This can be expensive, but may be worthwhile if you are thinking of using the space for working, storing expensive equipment, or as a bedroom. Building your own may end up almost as costly, unless you are going for a fairly basic version. Think carefully about what you need, and how the shape, size, and style will work within the garden as a whole. You could devise a design

Mirabel Osler's narrow town garden includes enclosed spaces hidden from the rest of the garden.

Left: Her outdoor dining room is enclosed by plants —roses, kiwi vines, and clematis have been trained to create a leafy bower overhead, while sprays of the gorgeous *Buddleia alternifolia* tumble over from one side. Some shade around a dining table is good if you are planning lunches outside.

to incorporate a treasured architectural fragment or pair of salvaged French doors—a good builder should be able to realize your plans. A sensible halfway measure might be to customize one of the self-assembly shed kits advertised in the back of magazines. I have seen this done most successfully, with a wood-burning stove inside and a deck veranda with rocking chairs out front. Whatever you have in mind, check with your local municipality to see if you need to obtain planning permits before going ahead.

Siting your garden building is crucial. Do you want it to work as a decorative feature, or be hidden away for privacy? Is cool summer shade the main motive, or making the most of the morning or evening sun? Some traditional garden buildings were built on basic turntables so they could be rotated to follow the sun or avoid the wind. If you have space, a gap can be left behind the structure to screen an area for composting or storing pots.

Above: This little wooden summerhouse looks like a garden shed with the front cut out. Painted fresh pale blue with a white interior, it sits well in the landscape of this Dutch garden, and is a peaceful place to sit and read. Plants in pots look pretty ranged along the window ledges.

Top left and right: A simple wood and glass cube behind Jonathan Bell's city home has made an enviable modern outside office for his landscape design business. The desk is positioned in front of the floor-to-ceiling window, allowing a view out through the tree across the garden.

Main picture: Strung with tree lights and glass flowers, and sprawling with bougainvillea and roses, this arbor has been transformed into a magical space. It gives shade during the day, and at night becomes the focus for relaxed entertaining, with comfortable seating, low tables, and potted plants.

There is something magical about even the simplest garden building—just that short distance from the house seems to bring a respite from the pressures and worries of the world.

A gazebo may be little more than a few trellis panels nailed together to form a loose enclosure, but grown over with roses and fragrant plants it can become a romantic and magical place. Such features are often the venues for romantic assignations—in novels, if not in real life. Other garden structures develop into eccentric worlds of their own—fantasy places where adults, as much as children, can play. The furnishings can break all the rules that might apply inside the house: pure kitsch, country chintz, or painted junk—anything goes. Or they can follow the theme you have chosen for the garden—beach-hut simplicity for a seaside plot, or faded gothic grandeur in a woodland glade. A corrugated metal hut might be fitted out like a logger's cabin, while a chic modern office might have a glass roof, built-in shelves, computer terminal, and telephone.

There is something magical about even the simplest garden building—just that short distance from the house seems to bring a respite from the pressures and worries of the world. So when planning one, from an ornate summerhouse to a tiny little hut, let your imagination run wild. Delve deep into childhood memories and daydreams to devise a place that you can really call your own.

Garden buildings can provide a touch of humor in a garden.

Above: The corrugated metal shed (**left**) looks rather like an old-fashioned privy, while the little beach hut (**right**), painted fresh yellow and blue, adds to the breezy seaside feel of this pebble and gravel garden. It would make a fun changing room at the edge of a swimming pool. Small huts such as this are useful for storing lawnmowers and other unsightly tools, but, left empty, they can become secret children's dens.

Above and left: The "Sulking House" at Bryan's Ground was created as a fiftieth birthday present from one of the owners, Simon Dorrell, to the other, David Wheeler. Three gothic arches from a demolished nineteenth-century warehouse frame views out over the garden, while the height of the stepped gables makes the building a landmark within the overall design. The beds on each side of the grass approach have been planted in suitably dark and dramatic colors to highlight the theme. Far from being a gloomy place, however, the summerhouse is used by musicians who entertain visitors when the garden is open to the public.

water features

Make room for water when designing your garden, from a tiny brook or fountain to a naturalistic swimming pool or ambitious sculptural effects.

The sight and sound of water in a garden have a positive effect on our minds and spirits. Still clear expanses soothe the soul and create stunning reflections of leaves or sky, while fountains are more stimulating and seem to energize the air. Choose whatever your space, style, and budget will allow—but do choose something, because the presence of water almost always improves a garden.

Water can work as a mirror, a coolant, a humidifier, or to give added impact to a piece of sculpture. Its sound can mask road traffic and aircraft noise, or provide a focus for meditation. Water in a garden can range from a large swimming pool to a wildlife pond to a narrow stream or tiny bubble fountain. The style can be formal, naturalistic, or ultra-modern, using bright-colored plastic, glass, or stone.

To look and function at its best, a water feature needs to be carefully planned within the overall design of the garden. Water needs to be integrated into the structure, not placed upon the surface. Too often, inspired by garden makeover programs on television, people seem to rush out and buy a fountain and pump before they have even decided where in their yard the water will go. Sometimes these small, self-contained units are the only option in a garden, but unless carefully treated, they can look like superfluous ornaments, cluttering up the space. Make your water feature as large as you can—you won't regret it.

Major features such as swimming pools and large ponds are not for everyone; they need to be professionally installed, and thought must be given to make them sit well in the garden's overall design.

Mounds of white glass chips rise like surreal pyramids from a pool in this glittering glass garden in California. The owner and designer, Andy Cao, created them as an evocation of his childhood in Vietnam, where piles of salt were left to dry in the open air. Most dramatic in the dawn light, they are among the many remembered or imagined images of Vietnam that Cao has incorporated into this unusual garden.

Right: Glass bricks, concrete, pebbles, and glass—a variety of modern materials has been employed to create this small water feature in a roof terrace by Stephen Woodhams. The semi-industrial aesthetic sits well with the bare brick wall behind and the galvanized metal grill on which the trough stands. The splashing or trickling of water is always welcome, even on a small roof terrace. In a city garden, it can help screen the noise of passing traffic or aircraft—but make sure it isn't loud enough to drown out conversation.

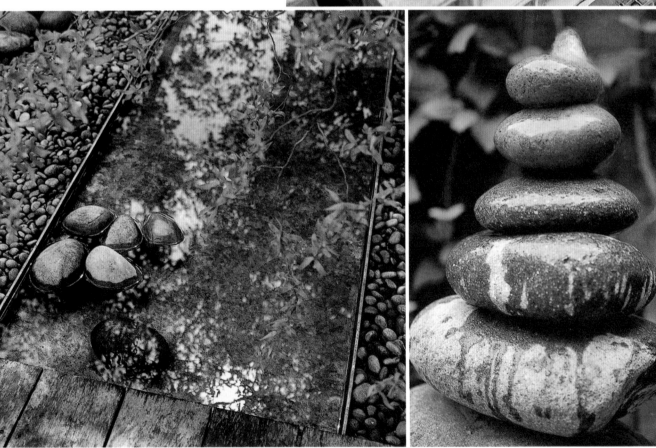

Others, such as hot tubs and outdoor showers, which are becoming increasingly fashionable, are more easily incorporated into even the smallest balconies and backyards. Few things can beat a shower in the sunshine or under the stars at night, and to sit in hot bubbling water looking down on a city or out to sea is a magical way to end the day. Screening can be provided by tall swishing plants like bamboos or by simple stylish structures in painted wood or sand-blasted glass.

Ponds or small pools work best when there is some movement in the water to stop it from growing stagnant and smelly, and for this you will need a submersible pump. Solar versions are available, but most only work when the sun is out. With an electric pump, which circulates water from the lowest point or reservoir to where it is needed and back again, you can create many different effects with water: a gently brimming vessel spilling water over its edges; a single jet of water in a geometric pond; or a starkly modern spout made from a sawn-off steel joist tipping water into a raised galvanized tank. Hide the switch somewhere near the house—if visitors see you turn on the pump, it will ruin the effect.

Far left: Just an inch or two of water in a galvanized metal trough can transform a garden. This stream may be small and shallow, but the cooling presence of water and the reflections on its surface soften the architecture of this modern roof garden and infinitely enhance its atmosphere.

Center: A hole can be drilled into a boulder, or a stack of stones, to make room for plumbing for a simple water feature. When the pump is turned off, the stones work as sculpture.

Below: A round pool with a simple stone border breaks up an expanse of lawn and mirrors the pattern of overhanging branches against the sky.

When it comes to materials, what you choose will reflect not only your budget, but also the style of your garden. Modern and formal pools look good with simple borders made of limestone blocks, gray slate, or pale stone. Wildlife ponds and more naturalistic features might use pebbles, flat stones, or gravel. Advances in the use of plants to clean and filter water mean that "swimming ponds," which look like natural lakes, are now a naturalistic alternative to the bright blue chlorinated pool. With all ponds and pools, make sure adequate safety measures are included—most places require pools to be securely fenced.

If you want a pool mainly for its reflections, use a dark liner or cover the inside with black tiles or paint. Floating islands and the reflections of brightly colored plants will combine to create an effect like an abstract painting in summer. In winter, even a cold cloudy sky will create a patch of pale gray beauty. And if it's icy, a shallow pool can be turned into an impromptu skating rink.

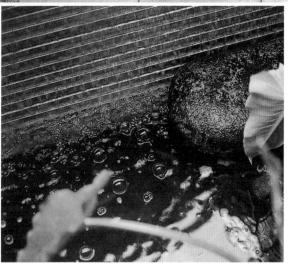

The dark narrow well outside a basement window has been transformed into a stunning water garden by architect Dale Loth. These basement areas are common in English town houses and can prove difficult to deal with. Here, some initial excavation work was needed to dig out the high retaining walls and create a wider, lighter, and more welcoming space that connects with the rest of the garden. The basement now opens onto a Japanese-inspired pond planted with arum lilies, creeping cotoneaster, and bamboo. Concrete paving stones and beach pebbles set in concrete lead to a flight of metal steps that give the impression of walking on water and lead up to the garden itself. All along one side, water trickles gently down a customized sheet of stainless steel, creating attractive sound and light effects, and helping to keep the water in the pond fresh.

With an electric pump, you can create many different effects with water: a gently brimming vessel spilling water over its edges; a single jet in a geometric pond; or a starkly modern spout made from a sawn-off steel joist tipping water into a raised galvanized tank.

groundworks

Define the different spaces in your garden with contemporary materials that work with the plants. Give traditional elements like stone, slate, and brick a modern twist, or experiment with wooden decking or industrial metal grates. Or for a cutting-edge look, go for textured concrete or colored glass chips.

Choosing the materials for the flooring and structure of your garden is probably the most important decision you will make. Inside, a good or bad floor surface can make or break a room, and the same is true outdoors. The right colors and textures for paving, steps, and retaining walls will not only complement the house and its surroundings, they will also establish the entire look and feel of the garden, and provide an attractive backdrop against which its other features can be seen to good advantage.

There are no hard and fast rules. Traditional materials such as brick and quarried stone tend to look happiest with period buildings, but a twist—using indigo-blue engineering bricks, or machine-cut stone with sharp edges—brings these centuries-old components up to date. And modern innovations like poured concrete and colored glass chips can

Main picture and center: This extraordinary California garden created by Andy Cao uses resin-bonded glass chips underfoot and heaped into sculptural mounds. The glass was tumbled to remove the sharp edges, and meticulously mixed and raked to create subtle transitions from one color to the next. Even the wall glitters, too, with blue-green and brown glass mixed into the concrete. Cao had to experiment with the planting, because glare from the glass can scorch delicate foliage.

Far left: For a slightly more traditional look, tiles, bricks, and clay pavers can be laid in all sorts of decorative patterns. The advantage of smaller units over larger paving stones is that they can be used to create curves and unusual shapes. Terra cotta weathers quickly, and tends to attract moss and self-seeding plants in the cracks. While this is attractive in a period property, slate or industrial engineering bricks would be more suited to a clean-edged modern look. Avoid using cheap new bricks if you can; they will always look cheap and new.

The paint colors used at the front of a house can contribute to the impact of the garden.

Right: Terra cotta and verdigris are a successful combination, and associate well with the climbers around the door.

Far right and below right: A purple picket fence matches the front door, while a duller grayish shade, used for the window frames, provides a foil for the different lavenders in the large windowbox and raised brick bed. The gate was moved a few feet to the left during a garden redesign to make an interesting angled route to the front door. The stone path is edged with purplish-gray slate chips.

Traditional materials such as brick and quarried stone tend to look happiest with period buildings, but a twist brings these centuries-old components up to date.

create surreal artistic environments that turn convention on its head.

Just as it does in a successful interior, a strong, simple floor treatment can bind the various elements of a garden together, leading the eye from one area of interest to another. This can be a good way of bringing unity to an established garden that is too good to dismantle, yet feels disparate. At other times, a more complex patterned effect may be exactly what is needed to "lift" a formal design composed from clipped plants and hedges, or to give focus to an uninteresting corridor or courtyard. Avoid using too many different materials and textures within the same area, however. Create graphic patterns using two different materials—stone with a contrasting brick border, or decking with a stone surround—or using a single component, such as pebbles for a mosaic, in just two or three shades.

The construction materials used in your garden should fulfill three vital criteria: they have to look right, they have

Above: California gardens such as this one are often built on steeply sloping hillsides, and consist of a series of terraces linked by steps and low stone or concrete retaining walls.

Below and opposite below left: In gardens with a relaxed and romantic feel, the weathering of stone and brick floors adds greatly to the atmosphere. Baby's tears (*Soleirolia soleirolii*) has spread among the cracks between stone pavers (**opposite**), while moss and ivy contribute to the pattern of the brick and cobblestone path (**below**). Maintenance may be necessary to stop the plants from taking over.

to feel right, and they have to be practical, particularly in areas of heavy use or where children will be playing. It makes sense to transfer the elements of your interior design style outdoors. If you are lucky enough to have large French doors opening off a living room or kitchen, think about continuing the same hard flooring surface to the area just outside the house—this looks great in summer when the doors are flung open all day. If you have used galvanized metal for fixtures or features, that, too, can come outside in the form of industrial metal grates for steps or walkways, or shiny tubs and planters.

Wooden decking looks good with almost any style of architecture, but salvaged railroad ties look best around converted warehouses or factories, or alongside wild and woodland planting. Consider color, texture, and the way the components' shapes would look over small and large areas, and as part of a pattern.

In a decorated garden, the feel of materials is almost as important as their visual impact. Do you want the cool, smooth texture of sandstone underfoot, or the scrunch of gravel or pebbles? The gentle heat of sun-warmed wood or the thrill of shiny buffed concrete? The right choice can bring an unexpectedly sensual element into the garden, and make walking around it a journey for all the senses.

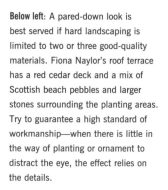

Below left: A pared-down look is best served if hard landscaping is limited to two or three good-quality materials. Fiona Naylor's roof terrace has a red cedar deck and a mix of Scottish beach pebbles and larger stones surrounding the planting areas. Try to guarantee a high standard of workmanship—when there is little in the way of planting or ornament to distract the eye, the effect relies on the details.

Above, above left, and right: The landscape designer Jonathan Bell's backyard displays similar restraint in materials and design. The open square trellis, sparse planting, and stone slabs in the pebbles create an understated Japanese feel. Adding a glass-roofed kitchen extension to the rear of the apartment created a wonderful indoor–outdoor dining space, but made the tiny yard even smaller. But by keeping things simple using just pebbles, stone, and concrete, Bell has retained some feeling of space and created a truly low-maintenance garden that requires, he says, just a couple of hours work a year. A shallow flight of steps leads to an upper terrace and a glass box of an office behind the kitchen—a small recess in the concrete **(above)** becomes a barbecue with the addition of a metal grill.

Right and far right: Stepping stones laid in gravel suit the minimalist style of Jonathan Bell's backyard. They were also a device used in Japanese gardens to slow down visitors on their route around a garden and bring them to a meditative state.

Below: Colored pigment was mixed with concrete to form the striking pink steps and mauve retaining walls in Judy Kameon's California garden. The colors are developing with time and weathering, creating attractive abstract effects that complement the textures of the planting.

In a decorated garden, the feel of materials is almost as important as visual impact. The right choice can bring a sensual element into the garden, and make walking around it a journey for all the senses.

Right: Galvanized metal is an increasingly popular material for modern gardens. Its semi-industrial appearance suits the urban aesthetic, and it is particularly useful in situations where a strong but partially transparent surface is needed. Here in Dale Loth's garden, metal steps add an exciting dynamic to a contemporary water feature. Bolted to the side wall, the slatted steps appear to float above the shallow pool, creating the effect of walking on water. Metal has also been used for the waterfall behind—a ridged stainless-steel sheet attached to the rear retaining wall has water trickling down its entire length. The natural organic forms of pebbles and boulders provide a welcome change in shape and texture. Galvanized metal is also ideal for balconies and terraces where light is required to pass through to the rooms beneath. It can also be laid just below the surface of a pool to create modern water features that are safe for children.

Practicalities must not be forgotten, of course. Will this surface stand the test of time and constant use? Will age add to its appeal or will it simply become scruffy? What sort of maintenance will it need? Will garden furniture stand on it without wobbling? All these aspects and more must be considered—this is probably the most expensive and permanent element of your garden's design, so it pays dividends to get it right from the start.

Wooden decks and paths have become extremely popular in recent years. Decking is reasonably cheap and easy to install, and looks good in a wide range of settings. Pine is inexpensive, but the irregularities in the grain can create a somewhat rustic finish—reclaimed scaffold boards are sturdy and give a more urban, semi-industrial feel. Iroko is great for roof gardens—its rich honey color turns a lovely silver gray if left to weather in the sun, but can be retained with regular oiling. Western red cedar is also a good choice for decks. It responds well to color-staining, but also weathers attractively naturally. Choose wood from sustainable sources. Decking is not without its problems, however, and it's not as low maintenance as you might think. Left untreated, the surface can become slippery in winter, and can gather a coat of lime-green algae in the shade. This can be removed by professional pressure-cleaning, or brushing by hand with a weak bleach solution and hosing down every spring.

Main picture: Wide shallow steps act rather like terracing, making for a gentle ascent in this California garden. The chunky wood risers infilled with gravel create a slightly rustic look that goes well with the naturalistic planting. Wispy grasses and nasturtiums spill onto the path, which is lit by candles in blue glass holders at night. This is a good use for salvaged railroad ties.

Center right: Even the most unexpected materials can create stunning decorative effects. At Bryan's Ground, sticks picked up by the owners' dogs provide the infill for a modern parterre in front of the house. Other compartments contain shattered slate and flat stones.

Far right: Pebbles are often used to bring a naturalistic feel to a modern garden. Here, Dale Loth has gone for a more formal look, laying similar-sized pebbles on end in concrete to create an attractive fishscale effect.

A strong, simple floor treatment can bind the garden together. Create graphic patterns using two different materials—stone with a brick border, or decking with a stone surround—or using a single component, such as pebbles for a mosaic, in just two or three shades.

You'll need to sweep your deck regularly to keep it looking shipshape—and make sure the gaps between the slats are not too large or you'll collect all sorts of debris underneath.

Pebbles and chips—stone, slate, marble, plastic, glass—are also popular materials in modern gardens. Pebbles can be bought in different shades and sizes—the larger they are, the more uncomfortable they are to walk over. Small Scottish beach pebbles in shades of soft pink, cream, and gray are an attractive alternative to gravel, and associate well with water and architectural plants like bamboo. Gravel and chips have long been used for driveways and decorative parterres, but have only recently taken pride of place in

the garden itself. Plain gray gravel or pea gravel looks great with Mediterranean-style plantings, where stray plants can self-seed easily and blur the edges of paths and beds. To complement a period house, try to use local chips that share the tones of the stone used in nearby buildings—Cotswold stone chips, for instance, have a lovely warm honey color and look good with cottage-garden plants. Slate chips, which come in a number of interesting shades from greenish gray to deep purple, are fun to use in a modern design, while black and white gravel used in segregated areas can create dramatic contrasts. Colored glass chips that have been tumbled to remove sharp edges can be used as decorative mulches for planters or retained beds, or piled in impressionistic heaps— as in Andy Cao's Los Angeles garden.

Pebbles and gravel don't just look good, however. If you lay a thick enough layer, they will retain moisture and keep down weeds. Their familiar scrunch beneath feet or car wheels can also be a helpful security signal. Their main drawbacks are that small components may spread where they're not wanted unless there is some small retaining wall—and that young children and pets may want to scoop them up or eat them. Fallen leaves will spoil that precious, pristine look, so watch what you plant unless you're prepared to gather them up by hand.

Stone slabs and pavers are a more traditional choice, and there are now attractive, inexpensive alternatives to quarried stone. Even concrete pavers can look good laid in an interesting pattern with enough gaps left in between for moss or baby's tears to add to the effect. For a circular terrace or curved pathway, wedge-shaped pavers make it easy to create a smooth flowing effect, while smaller granite slabs can be laid in decorative patterns or used to make an edging between planting and a lawn. Bricks always look good and weather quickly. Choose high-fired engineering bricks for a modern look or reclaimed bricks to match your

Main picture, top left, and left: The pattern of farms seen from the air inspired Isabelle Greene's design of this remarkable California garden. Concrete retaining walls divide the arid hillside plot into a series of terraces—making the molds from split cedar planks has given the concrete an interesting organic texture (**left**). Filled with colorful, low-growing plants and huge agaves, the beds look like a patchwork quilt.

Above and right: Traditional dry-laid stone wall techniques create a most nontraditional feature. Roberto Silva's swooping slate wall is more aesthetic than practical, though it does divide and define the garden's main areas—lawn, stone terrace, deck—and it can also be a seat.

The ultimate material for modern gardens, concrete is a chameleon that adapts to your dreams, becoming whatever you want it to be.

Bold planting works well partnered with equally bold modern colors and building materials.

Above left: The subtle shades of lavender, dark aeoniums, and low-growing succulent plants sit well against the textured pinkish concrete in this garden designed by Isabelle Greene. The California climate makes permanent outdoor plantings of tender plants possible.

Above right: A bubblegum-pink fence is the perfect backdrop for birds-of-paradise (*Strelitzia*) in Andy Cao's glass garden. Imagine it when the bright orange and blue flowers come out.

Main picture: A cascade of nasturtiums in every shade of yellow and orange sets off the blue-gray concrete of these steps leading up to garden designer Judy Horton's house in Los Angeles.

house, but avoid cheap new bricks—they will always look cheap and new. Bricks lend themselves to pattern-making, but just a single line of contrasting brick between areas of paving transforms a dull path or terrace.

One of the most exciting materials for modern gardens is poured concrete. Incorporate it early in the planning stage, and it can create paths and steps, retain beds and terraces, and make dramatic changes in level. The surface can be buffed smooth like polished stone, brushed while drying to expose the aggregate, colored, or imprinted with interesting textures. Perhaps the ultimate material for the contemporary garden, concrete is a chameleon that can adapt to your dreams, becoming whatever you want it to be.

Directory

GARDEN FURNITURE AND ACCESSORIES

B&B Italia
150 East 58th Street
New York
NY 10155
(800) 872-1697
www.bebitalia.it
Italian modern classics.

Crate & Barrel
For your nearest store
(800) 927-9202
www.crateandbarrel.com
Outdoor dinnerware, furniture, and accessories.

Design Within Reach
283 Fourth Street Oakland
CA 94607
(800) 944-2233
www.designwithinreach. com
Stylish furniture, including outdoor benches, chairs, and loungers.

Florentine Craftsmen
46-24 28th Street
Long Island City
NY 11101
(718) 937-7632
www.florentinecraftsmen. com
Classic furniture, fountains, statuary, planters, and urns.

Plow & Hearth
P.O. Box 6000
Madison
VA 22727
(800) 494-7544
www.plowhearth.com
Furniture, cushions, all-weather wicker, outdoor fireplaces, and lanterns.

Pottery Barn
Stores nationwide
(888) 779-5176
www.potterybarn.com
Tables, chairs, and a variety of garden ornamentation.

Mary Rawlinson
1 Bower Gardens
Salisbury
Wiltshire SP1 2RL
UK
(+44) 1722 321745
One-off commissions in oak. Made the seat shown on p64.

Restoration Hardware
For your nearest store
(800) 816-0969
www.restorationhardware. com
Potting benches, garden accessories.

Target Stores
Stores nationwide
(888) 304-4000
www.target.com
Reasonably priced outdoor furniture—with a little flair.

Vermont Outdoor Furniture
9 Auburn Street
Barre
VT 05641
(800) 588-8834
www.vermontoutdoor furniture.com
Simple, beautiful wood seating, porch swings, gliders, tables.

Wood Classics
20 Osprey Lane
Gardiner
NY 12525
(845) 255-7871
Elegant, simple wood furniture: chairs, benches, gliders, umbrellas, and tables.

LIGHTING

Escort Lighting
(800) 856-7948
www.escortlighting.com
Outdoor lighting.

Lamps Plus
(800) 782-1967
www.lampsplus.com
Simple, functional landscape lighting.

Stone Manor Lighting
6219 Porterdale Drive
Malibu
CA 90265
(888) 534-0544
www.stonemanorlighting. com
Outdoor lighting with handmade copper and glass fixtures.

ART AND SCULPTURE

Adkins Architectural Antiques
3515 Fannin Street
Houston
TX 77004
(800) 522-6547
www.adkinsantiques.com
Gargoyles and griffins and other grand garden ornaments.

Angela Conner
(+44) 20 7221 4510
Kinetic water sculptures.

Garden Accents
4 Union Hill Road
West Conshohocken
PA 19428
(800) 296-5525
www.garden-accent.com
Antiques, backyard habitat, benches, statuary, water features, lighting, sundials, planters, and urns.

Glasshouse Works
P.O. Box 97
Church Street
Stewart
OH 45778-0097
(800) 837-2142
www.graniteisforever.com
Granite obelisks, orbs, and dragons.

Meridian Landscape Art
P.O. Box 5633
Traverse City
MI 49696
(231) 947-6400
www.meridian-landscape-art.com
Landscape art, sculpture, and planters.

William Pye
(+44) 20 8682 2727
Master of modern water sculpture.

Joe Smith
Prestige Stoneworks
Milton
Crocketford
Dumfries DG2 8RJ
UK
(+44) 1556 690632
Made Mirabel Osler's urn, featured on p79.

Stone Forest
P.O. Box 2840
Santa Fe
NM 87504
(505) 986-8883
www.stoneforest.com
Hand-carved granite sculpture in Japanese and contemporary styles. Also basins, fountains, functional sculpture, stepping stones.

CONTAINERS

Bluestone Perennials
7211 Middle Ridge Road
Madison
OH 44057-3096
(800) 852-5243
www.bluestoneperennials. com
Perennials, plants, herbs, ornamental shrubs, and bulbs.

Charleston Gardens
61 Queen Street
Charleston
SC 29401
(800) 469-0118
www.charlestongardens. com
Planters and jardinieres, but also lighting, garden features, and fountains.

Gardener's Supply Company
128 Intervale Road
Burlington
VT 05401
(888) 833-1412
Lightweight planters, as well as obelisks, willow fences and borders, trellises, and statuary.

Martha by Mail
P.O. Box 60060
Tampa
FL 33660
(800) 950-7130
www.marthabymail.com
*Classy containers
and ornaments.*

Seibert & Rice
P.O. Box 365
Short Hills
NJ 07078
(973) 467-8266
www.seibert-rice.com
*Exquisite terra cotta, pots,
troughs, and urns.*

Smith & Hawken
35 Corte Madera Avenue
Mill Valley
CA 94941
(800) 940-1170
www.smith-hawken.com
*Simple and classic
containers. Also garden
structure, trellises, arches,
obelisks, fountains, gates,
fencing, ornaments,
sculpture, and topiary
forms.*

DECORATIVE PLANT SUPPORTS

Garden Arches
P.O. Box 4057
Bellingham
WA 98227
(800) 947-7697
www.gardenarches.com
*Arches, trellises, and
tuteurs in cedar, copper,
and iron.*

Walt Nicke's Garden Talk
P.O. Box 433
Topsfield
MA 01983
(978) 887-3388
www.gardentalk.com
*Arches, obelisks, and
gazebos, as well as fine
tools and
garden ornaments.*

Sycamore Creek
P.O. Box 16
Ancram
NY 12502
(518) 398-6393
www.sycamorecreek.com
*Copper garden furnishings:
arbors, trellises,
ornaments, chairs,
benches, tables.*

Trellis Structures
60 River Street
Beverly
MA 01915
(888) 285-4624
www.trellisstructures.com
*Arbors and trellises
from traditional to
contemporary; pergolas,
chairs, and benches.*

TOPIARY

FrenchWyres
P.O. Box 131655
Tyler
TX 75713
(903) 561-1742
www.frenchwyres.com
*Wirework arches, trellises,
urns, baskets, containers,
furniture, tables, chairs,
planters, obelisks, and
tuteurs.*

Kinsman Company
P.O. Box 428
Pipersville
PA 18947
(800) 733-4146
www.kinsmangarden.com
*Moss-lined baskets, topiary
forms, hooks, and wreath
rings.*

SUMMERHOUSES AND RETREATS

Richard Craven
Church Cottage
Stoke St Milborough.
Ludlow
Shropshire SY8 2EJ
UK
(+44) 1584 823631
*Made Mirabel Osler's 'Cat
House' on p112—also
makes treehouses, follies,
and summerhouses.*

Dalton Pavilions
20 Commerce Drive
Telford
PA 18969
(215) 721-1492
www.daltonpavilions.com
*Gazebos and other
garden structures.*

T Houses
P.O. Box 1235
Ojai
CA 93024
(805) 646-2421
www.tonysthouse.com
*Asian-inspired garden
structures for meditation,
relaxing, or reflection.*

Ben Wilson
78A Colneyhatch Lane
London N10 1EA
UK
(+44) 20 8444 3513
*Sculptor who can be
commissioned to make
one-off woodland walkways
and other structures.*

WATER FEATURES

Lilypons Water Gardens
6800 Lilypons Lane
P.O. Box 10
Buckeystown
MD 21717
www.lilypons.com
*Water gardening supplies,
as well as tropical lilies
and lotus.*

Paradise Water Gardens
14 May Street
Whitman
MA 02382
(800) 955-0161
www.
paradisewatergardens.com
*Fish, preformed ponds,
pond liners, fountains, and
waterfalls.*

Waterford Gardens
74 East Allendale Road
Saddle Rive
NJ 07458.
(201) 327-0721
www.waterfordgardens.
com
*Pond supplies, plants,
and fish.*

GROUNDWORKS

Ace Hardware Corporation
Stores nationwide
(630) 990-6600
www.acehardware.com
Hardware from A to Z.

The Home Depot
Stores nationwide
(800) 430-3376
www.homedepot.com
*Bricks, pavers, stone,
lumber, and hardware.*

Garden designers whose work is featured in this book:

Key: a=above, b=below, c=center, l=left, r=right

Jonathan Bell
11 Sinclair Gardens
London W14 0AU UK
t. +44 20 7371 3455
e. jb@jbell.demon.co.uk
Pages 120l, 114al 114ar, 128al, 128–129, 129, 130al, 130ar.

Susan Berger & Helen Phillips
Town Garden Design
69 Kingsdown Parade
Bristol BS6 5UG UK
t./f. +44 117 942 3843
Pages 62al, 65ar, 97cb, 101r, 102r, 106–107.

De Brinkhof Garden and Nursery
Dorpsstrat 46
6616 AJ Hernen Holland
t. +31 487 531 486
Nursery and garden open every Tuesday, Friday, & Saturday from 10am to 5pm, from April until the end of September.
A small nursery specializing in old-fashioned and unusual varieties of hardy perennial.
Pages 96, 98br, 114b, 124al, 124bl.

Bryan's Ground Garden Design
t. +44 1544 260001
Pages 1, 80l, 85r, 99, 104l, 117, 133l.

Andrew Cao
Glass Garden Inc.
1626 Fargo Street
Los Angeles
CA 90026
t. 323 666 2727
f. 323 666 2791
e. glassgarden@earthlink.net
www.glassgardendesign.com
Pages 83c, 92br, 118–119, 124ar, 125, 136r.

Nellie Christiaans & Manus Hijmans' Garden & Nursery
Haneman 9
6645 CA Winssen Holland
t. +31 487 522 231
Garden and plant nursery specializing in clipped boxwood and sedums. Please call if you wish to visit the nursery.
Pages 62ar, 91bl, 95, 108–109, 110ar.

Cooper/Taggart Designs
t. 323 254 3048
e. coopertaggart@earthlink.net
Pages 4, 52–53, 59r, 67bl, 67br, 68al, 69, 80r, 83b, 92l, 115, 132.

Isabelle C. Greene, F.A.S.L.A.
Isabelle Greene & Associates
Landscape Architects and Land Planners
2613 De La Vina Street
Santa Barbara
CA 93105
t. 805 569 4045
e. icgreene@aol.com
Pages 60–61, 76–77, 79, 88l, 89, 94b, 134a, 134b, 134–135, 136b.

Ivan Hicks
Garden and Landscape Designer, Land Artist
t./f. +44 1963 210886
e. ivan@theedge88.fsnet.co.uk
Pages 85al, 85bl.

Judy M. Horton, Garden Design
136 1/2 North Larchmont Boulevard, Suite B
Los Angeles
CA 9004
t. 323 462 1412
f. 323 462 8979
e. info@jmhgardendesign.com
Pages 2–3, 22–27, 104r, 105, 110l, 137.

Jan Howard
Room in the Garden
Oak Cottage
Furzen Lane
Ellens Green, Rudgwick
West Sussex RH12 3AR UK
t. +44 1403 823958
Manufacturers of elegant designs in rusted iron. Garden design services by Jan Howard. Catalog available.
Pages 84, 94a, 97l, 98ar, 100.

Johnson-Naylor Interior Architecture
t. +44 20 7490 8885
Pages Front endpapers, 8–9, 16–21, 40–45, 54, 55al, 55ar, 55bl, 120bl, 128bl.

Judy Kameon
Elysian Landscapes
724 Academy Road
Los Angeles
CA 90012
t. 323 226 9588
f. 323 226 1191
www.plainair.com
Garden design and outdoor furniture.
Pages 56–58, 59l, 74, 90, 127a, 130b.

Dale Loth Architects
1 Cliff Road
London NW1 9AJ UK
t. +44 20 7485 4003
f. +44 20 7284 4490
e. mail@dalelotharchitects.co.uk
Pages 122–123, 131, 133r.

Lucy Moore
Garden Designer
Pages 103l, 116l, 126al.

Christina Oates
Secret Garden Designs
Fovant Hut
Fovant
nr. Salisbury
Wiltshire SP3 5LN UK
t. +44 1722 714756
www.secretgardendesigns.co.uk
Garden designer Christina Oates specializes in imaginative and yet down-to-earth consultancy visits and concept plans.
Pages 64, 86b.

Nancy Goslee Power & Associates
1660 Stanford Street
Santa Monica
CA 90904
t. 310 264 0266
f. 310 264 0268
e. ngpa@nancypower.com
Pages 7, 16–21.

Sarah Raven's Cutting Garden
Perch Hill Farm
Brightling
Robertsbridge
East Sussex TN32 5HP UK
t. +44 1424 838181
f. +44 1424 838571
e. info@thecuttinggarden.com
www.thecuttinggarden.com
Pages 65ac, 65b, 98l, 102c, 103r, 110al, 121.

Suzanne Rheinstein Associates
817 North Hilldale Avenue
West Hollywood
CA 90069
t. 323 931 340
Hollyhock Hilldale
Address as above
Garden antiques & accessories.
e. Hollyhockinc@aol.com
Pages 2–3, 22–27.

Marc Schoellen
35 route de Colmar-Berg
L-7525 Mersch
Grand-Duché de Luxembourg
t. +352 327 269
Garden historian & amateur garden designer.
Pages 63al, 86al, 97r, 111.

Roberto Silva
567 Wandsworth Road
London SW8 3JD UK
t. +44 20 7498 9675
e. landrob7@aol.com
Pages 46–51, 78–79, 135bl, 135br, back endpapers.

Sally Storey
John Cullen Lighting
585 Kings Road
London SW6 2EH UK
t. +44 20 7371 5400
A wide range of practical contemporary light fittings as well as innovative made-to-measure lighting design.
Pages 70–71, 78al, 120br.

Tom Stuart-Smith
3rd Floor
Kirkman House
12–14 Whitfield Street
London W1P 5RD UK
Pages 55br, 65al.

Whitelaw Turkington
Landscape Architects
t. +44 20 7820 0388
Pages Front endpapers, 8–9, 40–45, 54, 55al, 55ar, 55bl, 120bl, 128bl.

Stephen Woodhams
Unit 3
McKay Trading Estate
248–300 Kensal Road
London W10 5BZ UK
t. +44 20 8964 9818
Pages 72–73, 91al, 91ar, 91br, 120a.

Picture credits

Key: a=above, b=below, c=center, l=left, r=right

All photographs by Melanie Eclare

Front endpapers Fiona Naylor and Peter Marlow's roof garden in London designed by Fiona Naylor and landscape architect Lindsey Whitelaw; 1 Bryan's Ground, David Wheeler and Simon Dorrell's garden in Herefordshire; 2–3 garden of interior designer Suzanne Rheinstein, designed by Judy M. Horton; 4 Laura Cooper & Nick Taggart's Los Angeles garden designed by Cooper/Taggart Designs; 5 Elspeth Thompson's garden in south London; 7 Nancy Goslee Power, garden designer; 8–9 Fiona Naylor and Peter Marlow's roof garden in London designed by Fiona Naylor and landscape architect Lindsey Whitelaw; 10–15 Elspeth Thompson's garden in south London; 16–21 Nancy Goslee Power, garden designer; 22–27 garden of interior designer Suzanne Rheinstein, designed by Judy M. Horton; 28–33 Hutton Wilkinson's garden designed by Tony Duquette; 34–39 Mirabel Osler's garden in Ludlow, Shropshire; 40–45 Fiona Naylor and Peter Marlow's roof garden in London designed by Fiona Naylor and landscape architect Lindsey Whitelaw; 46–51 a garden in south London designed by Roberto Silva; 52–53 Laura Cooper & Nick Taggart's Los Angeles garden designed by Cooper/Taggart Designs: 54, 55 al, 55ar, & 55bl Fiona Naylor and Peter Marlow's roof garden in London designed by Fiona Naylor and landscape architect Lindsey Whitelaw; 55br Tom Stuart-Smith's garden in Herefordshire; 56–58 & 59l Judy Kameon's garden in Los Angeles–designer & owner of Elysian Landscapes; 59r Laura Cooper & Nick Taggart's Los Angeles garden designed by Cooper/Taggart Designs; 60–61 Carol Valentine's garden in California, designed by Isabelle Greene, F.A.S.L.A., a California landscape architect and planner; 62al the garden of James Morris in Bristol designed by Sue Berger & Helen Phillips; 62ar Nellie Christiaans & Manus Hijmans' garden & nursery in Winssen, Holland; 62b & 63b Niall Manning & Alastair Morton's garden, Dunard, Fintry, Scotland G63 0EX; 63al Marc Schoellen's garden, 'La Bergerie,' in Luxembourg; 63ar Mirabel Osler's garden in Ludlow, Shropshire; 64 Fovant Hut Garden near Salisbury in Wiltshire was created by garden designer Christina Oates together with her husband Nigel and is open to the public; 65al Tom Stuart-Smith's garden in Herefordshire; 65ac & b Sarah Raven's Cutting Garden in Brightling, designed by Sarah Raven; 65ar Sue Berger's garden in Bristol designed by Sue Berger; 66 & 67a Elspeth Thompson's garden in south London; 67bl, br, & 68al Laura Cooper & Nick Taggart's Los Angeles garden designed by Cooper/Taggart Designs; 68ac, ar, & b Elspeth Thompson's garden in south London; 69 Laura Cooper & Nick Taggart's Los Angeles garden designed by Cooper/Taggart Designs; 70–71 a house in Chelsea, lighting designed by Sally Storey; 72–73 Sarah Harrison & Jamie Hodder-Williams's roof terrace in London designed by Stephen Woodhams; 74 garden designed by Judy Kameon–Elysian Landscapes; 75 Elspeth Thompson's garden in south London; 76–77 Carol Valentine's garden in California, designed by Isabelle Greene, F.A.S.L.A., a California landscape architect and planner; 78al a house in Chelsea, lighting designed by Sally Storey; 78bl Mirabel Osler's garden in Ludlow, Shropshire; 78–79 a garden in south London designed by Roberto Silva; 79 Carol Valentine's garden in California, designed by Isabelle Greene, F.A.S.L.A., a California landscape architect and planner; 80l Bryan's Ground, David Wheeler and Simon Dorrell's garden in Herefordshire; 80r Laura Cooper & Nick Taggart's Los Angeles garden designed by Cooper/Taggart Designs; 81l Hutton Wilkinson's garden designed by Tony Duquette; 81r Mirabel Osler's garden in Ludlow, Shropshire; 82l Elspeth Thompson's garden in south London; 82r & 83a Hutton Wilkinson's garden designed by Tony Duquette; 83c owners Steven Jerrom & Andrew Cao, landscape design by Andrew Cao; 83b Laura Cooper & Nick Taggart's Los Angeles garden designed by Cooper/Taggart Designs; 84 Jan Howard's garden in Sussex; 85al & bl Mart Barlow's garden designed by Ivan Hicks; 85r Bryan's Ground, David Wheeler and Simon Dorrell's garden in Herefordshire; 86al Marc Schoellen's garden, 'La Bergerie,' in Luxembourg; 86b Fovant Hut Garden near Salisbury in Wiltshire was created by garden designer Christina Oates together with her husband Nigel and is open to the public; 86ar & 87 Farrell Family garden, Woodnewton; 88r Elspeth Thompson's garden in south London; 88l & 89 Carol Valentine's garden in California, designed by Isabelle Greene, F.A.S.L.A., a California landscape architect and planner; 90 garden designed by Judy Kameon–Elysian Landscapes; 91al, ar, & br Sarah Harrison & Jamie Hodder-Williams's roof terrace in London designed by Stephen Woodhams; 91bl Nellie Christiaans & Manus Hijmans' garden & nursery in Winssen, Holland; 92l Laura Cooper & Nick Taggart's Los Angeles garden designed by Cooper/Taggart Designs; 92ar the garden of James Morris in Bristol designed by Sue Berger & Helen Phillips; 92br owners Steven Jerrom & Andrew Cao, landscape design by Andrew Cao; 93 Elspeth Thompson's garden in south London; 94a Jan Howard's garden in Sussex; 94b Carol Valentine's garden in California, designed by Isabelle Greene, F.A.S.L.A., a California landscape architect and planner; 95 Nellie Christiaans & Manus Hijmans' garden & nursery in Winssen, Holland; 96 the garden and nursery De Brinkhof of Riet Brinkhof & Joop Van Den Berk; 97l Jan Howard's garden in Sussex; 97ca Niall Manning & Alastair Morton's garden, Dunard, Fintry, Scotland G63 0EX; 97cb the garden of James Morris in Bristol designed by Sue Berger & Helen Phillips; 97r Marc Schoellen's garden, 'La Bergerie,' in Luxembourg; 98l Sarah Raven's Cutting Garden in Brightling, designed by Sarah Raven; 98ar Jan Howard's garden in Sussex; 98br the garden and nursery De Brinkhof of Riet Brinkhof & Joop Van Den Berk; 99 Bryan's Ground, David Wheeler and Simon Dorrell's garden in Herefordshire; 100 Jan Howard's garden in Sussex; 101l garden designer Judy M. Horton's garden in California; 101r & 102r Sue Berger's garden in Bristol designed by Sue Berger; 102l a garden in London designed by Jonathan Bell; 102c & 103r Sarah Raven's Cutting Garden in Brightling, designed by Sarah Raven; 103l garden designer Lucy Moore's own garden in Bristol; 104l Bryan's Ground, David Wheeler and Simon Dorrell's garden in Herefordshire; 104r & 105 garden designer Judy M. Horton's garden in California; 106–107 the garden of James Morris in Bristol designed by Sue Berger & Helen Phillips; 108–109 Nellie Christiaans & Manus Hijmans' garden & nursery in Winssen, Holland; 110al Sarah Raven's Cutting Garden in Brightling, designed by Sarah Raven; 110ar Nellie Christiaans & Manus Hijmans' garden & nursery in Winssen, Holland; 110b Farrell Family garden, Woodnewton; 111 Marc Schoellen's garden, 'La Bergerie,' in Luxembourg; 112bl Farrell Family garden, Woodnewton; 112al, 112r, & 113 Mirabel Osler's garden in Ludlow, Shropshire; 114al & ar a garden in London designed by Jonathan Bell; 114b the garden and nursery De Brinkhof of Riet Brinkhof & Joop Van Den Berk; 115 Laura Cooper & Nick Taggart's Los Angeles garden designed by Cooper/Taggart Designs; 116l garden designer Lucy Moore's own garden in Bristol; 116r Farrell Family garden, Woodnewton; 117 Bryan's Ground, David Wheeler and Simon Dorrell's garden in Herefordshire; 118–119 owners Steven Jerrom & Andrew Cao, landscape design by Andrew Cao; 120a Sarah Harrison & Jamie Hodder-Williams's roof terrace in London designed by Stephen Woodhams; 120bl Fiona Naylor and Peter Marlow's roof garden in London designed by Fiona Naylor and landscape architect Lindsey Whitelaw; 120br a house in Chelsea, lighting designed by Sally Storey; 121 Sarah Raven's Cutting Garden in Brightling, designed by Sarah Raven; 122–123 architect's house and garden in London designed by Dale Loth Architects; 124al & bl the garden and nursery De Brinkhof of Riet Brinkhof & Joop Van Den Berk; 124ar & 125 owners Steven Jerrom & Andrew Cao, landscape design by Andrew Cao; 126al garden designer Lucy Moore's own garden in Bristol; 126bl Janey Hall's Bristol garden; 126ar & 126br Elspeth Thompson's garden in south London; 127a garden designed by Judy Kameon–Elysian Landscapes; 127b Mirabel Osler's garden in Ludlow, Shropshire; 128bl Fiona Naylor and Peter Marlow's roof garden in London designed by Fiona Naylor and landscape architect Lindsey Whitelaw; 128al, 128–130al, & 130ar a garden in London designed by Jonathan Bell; 130b garden designed by Judy Kameon–Elysian Landscapes; 131 architect's house and garden in London designed by Dale Loth Architects; 132 Laura Cooper & Nick Taggart's Los Angeles garden designed by Cooper/Taggart Designs; 133l Bryan's Ground, David Wheeler and Simon Dorrell's garden in Herefordshire; 133r architect's house and garden in London designed by Dale Loth Architects; 134a, b, & 134–135 Carol Valentine's garden in California, designed by Isabelle Greene, F.A.S.L.A., a California landscape architect and planner; 135bl & br a garden in south London designed by Roberto Silva; 136l Carol Valentine's garden in California, designed by Isabelle Greene, F.A.S.L.A., a California landscape architect and planner; 136r owners Steven Jerrom & Andrew Cao, landscape design by Andrew Cao; 137 garden designer Judy M. Horton's garden in California; Back endpapers a garden in south London designed by Roberto Silva.

Figures in *italics* indicate captions.

INDEX

A

acanthus 12, *22*, 25
Aeonium arboreum 'Schwartzkopf'
  26, 94
aeoniums 27, *136*
agapanthus 19
agaves 33, *135*
alcoves *12*, 14
alliums 102
aloes *94*
arbors 58, 65, *101*, 68, 72, *101*,
  102, *102*, 114
arches *13*, 34, *35*, 101–2, *103*,
  117
armchairs 20, 55, 58, *62*
art and sculpture 76–87
awnings 54

B

B&B Italia *41*, 55
baby's tears *127*, 134
balconies 110, *131*
Balinese balls 33
balustrading *11*, *30*
bamboo 12, 42, *42*, *72*, *82*, 94,
  121, *123*
barbecues *129*
baskets *36*
baths, galvanized *97*
bay *72*, 106
beach huts *116*
beads, glass *66*, 105
bed springs *104*
beds 12, 19, 20, 54, 89, 90, *117*,
  133
  flower 48, 54, 90, 94, *103*, *104*,
    105, *111*
  raised *11*, 13, 20, *126*
  retained 134, 136
begonias 27
Bell, Jonathan *102*, *114*, *129*, *130*
benches 38, 56, 58, 62, *62*, *63*,
  65, *65*, 86
Berger, Sue *102*, 106
Bertoia, Harry 55
birch 42
birdbaths 86
birds-of-paradise *136*
bluestone 25, *25*
bottles *66*, *80*, 82, *83*, 84, *84*
bougainvilleas 77, *114*
boulders 51, *71*, *79*, 121, *131*
bowls *15*, 20, *74*, *79*, *88*, 97, 99
boxwood 25, 106, 110, 111

B

brick(s) 23, 25, *25*, *35*, 37, *120*,
  124, *125*, 127, 136
bromeliads 33
bronze 77
brooks 118
Bryan's Ground *80*, *98*, *117*, *132*
buckets 89, *89*, 91, 93, 97
Buddha statues *11*, *82*
Buddleia alternifolia 37, 113
builders' trough 98
bulbs 89, 90
Buxus 106

C

cacti 33, *92*
cairns 48, *49*, *71*, *79*
camellias 106
candles 6, *15*, 20, *20*, 48, *51*, 66,
  67, 68, *72*
Cao, Andy *83*, *118*, *125*, 134, *136*
capitals, Ionic 87
"Cat House" *113*
Cerinthe major 'Purpurascens' 90
chairs 16, 19, *20*, 54, 56, *62*,
  65, *68*
  basketweave 55
  bucket 54
  folding *12*, *35*, *37*, 55, 58, *62*
  metal *56*, 58, *59*
  planter's 65
  rocking 114
  topiary *109*
Chamaecyparis lawsoniana 106
chandeliers *20*, 84
cherry trees 7, *12*, 13, *47*, 48,
  51, *51*
Chinese elm *22*, 23
chips *83*, *92*, 94, *118*, 124, *125*,
  126, 127, 133–4
Christiaans, Nellie *109*
citrus trees *97*, *101*
clematis *13*, *35*, 37, 38, 101–2,
  102, 110, *113*
climbers 11, *11*, 13, *20*, 35, 36,
  38, *68*, *71*, 72, 89, 101, *101*,
  102, *102*, 104, 110, *126*
cobblestones *35*, 37
coleus *26*, 27
columns 30, *32*, 87
compost 93, *112*, 114
concrete 11, *120*, 124, *129*, *130*,
  131, 136, *136*
Conner, Angela 86
container gardening 93

C

containers 13, *25*, 26, *39*, 43, *75*,
  88–99, 106, 110
Convolvulus cneorum 13
Cooper, Laura *66*
cordylines *72*
corridors 16, 20, 34, 127
cotoneaster *123*
courtyards 16, 38, *68*, 89, 127
crassulas *92*, *94*
Craven, Richard 86, *113*
crocks 93
crocosmias *51*, *106*
cucumbers 102
cushions 6, 19, 54, 56, *56*, 59
  see also pillows
Cutting Garden, Sussex *103*
cypress
  Italian 38
  Lawson 106
  leyland 87

D

daffodils 90
Day, Robin 54, *55*
daybeds 59
decks 11, 12, *12*, *41*, *41*, 44, *45*,
  48, 56, 58, 72, 73, 127, 128,
  129, 131, 133, *135*
dimmer switches *72*
dining areas 38, *129*
doors 30, 34, *41*, *126*
  double 11
  false *35*, 37
  French 11, *11*, 13, *13*, 114, 128
  painted wooden 16
  temple 33
Dorrell, Stephen *117*
downlighters 70, *71*
driveways *72*, 133
Duquette, Elizabeth 29, 30
Duquette, Tony 29, 30, *80*, *83*

E

echeverias *94*
elaeagnus 42
Elaeagnus x ebbingei 42
empty spaces 27
entrances *72*
eucalyptus 30, 33, 38, 42, *42*, 51
Eucomis bicolor 13
euphorbias 12, *106*
evergreens *22*, 25, *26*, 38, 90,
  106

F

Farrell, Peter 87
Farrell family *112*
fences 37, 38, *39*, 126
feng shui 94
ferns 30, 33, *37*, 38, *39*, 43,
  51, *75*
fertilizer 93
Festuca glauca 51
fibre optics *72*
fig trees 94
figures 77, 81
Finlay, Ian Hamilton 78
fireplaces 6, 16, 19, *20*
flares 68
flooring 6
  geometric stone 16
  mosaic *16*, 20
  tiled-effect stone 19
  see also groundworks
flowerbeds 54, 90, *103*, *104*, 111
flowering maple *101*
flowers, glass *114*
follies 113
formal gardens 23, 25, 127
fountains 6, 19, 38, 48, 51, *72*,
  72, *74*, *79*, 97, 99, 118, 121
Fovant Hut Garden 65, *87*
French windows 11, *11*, 13, *13*,
  128
furniture 54–65

G

garden buildings 112–17
Garden of Cosmology, Scotland
  86–7
gates *94*
gazebos 116
glass jars 68
golden hops *101*
Goldsworthy, Andy *47*, 78
gourds *20*
grapevines *37*, 38, *66*, 102
grass(es) *22*, 23, 27, 42, 43, 109,
  110, *132*
  feather *83*
  ornamental 42, 90
  stipa 51
gravel 20, 23, 25, *25*, *47*, 48, *49*,
  71, *79*, *88*, 93, 94, *116*, 131,
  132, 133, 134
Greene, Isabel 77, *135*, *136*
greenhouses *111*
grates 124, 128

grillwork and grills 11, *11*, 12, *90*, *120*, *129*

groundworks 124–37

H

hats *36*

hawthorn 106, 109

heating 6

hedges 20, 42, *42*, 97, 106, *111*, 127

  box 25

  topiary *111*

hellebores 38

hens-and-chicks *93*

Hepworth, Barbara 78

herb gardens 97, 99

herbs 110

Hicks, Ian 79–80, 84

Hijmans, Manus *109*

holly 106

honeysuckle 101–2, *104*

Horton, Judy *136*

hostas 39, 41, 43

hot tubs 6, 121

Howard, Jan *84*, *104*

I

Iris reticulata 90

irises, flag 19

ivy 30, 33, *75*, *102*

J

jacuzzi 16, *16*, 19

Japanese gardens 47, *49*, 51, *79*, *130*

Jarman, Derek 80, 82

Jencks, Charles 86–7

juniper 38, 106

K

Kameon, Judy *56*, *59*, *130*

kinetic water sculptures 86

kiwi plants *37*, 38, 102, *113*

L

laburnum 102

lakes 87

lamiums *75*

lamps 71

  halogen *72*

lampshades *56*

lanterns *11*, *12*, 14, *15*, 51, 68, *68*, *72*, 74, *74*, *75*

Laurus nobilis 106

lavender 13, *62*, 89, 90, 106, *111*, *126*, *136*

lawns 6, 7, *22*, 25, *25*, 27, 48, 51, 54, 82, *84*, 97, 121, *135*

leyland cypresses 87

lighting 6, 66–75, 87

  underwater 19

lilies

  arum *123*

  pineapple *13*

  'Star Gazer' 20

lily ponds 19

linden trees *39*, *62*, *106*, 109

"Little Sparta," Scotland 78

loggia 16, 19, *20*

Long, Richard 78

Loth, Dale *123*, *131*, *132*

loungers 54, *55*, *56*

M

Macleaya cordata 12, *111*

manure 93

maples 51

marbles *83*

Metrosideros excelsus 20

mirrors 11, *12*, 14, 34, *37*, 38, *39*, 68, *72*, 80, *80*

morning glory *13*, 102

mosaic 16, 19, 20, *20*, *56*, *92*, 127, 133

moss 58, *90*, *125*

N

nasturtiums 13, 90, 102, *132*, *136*

Naylor, Fiona 41, 43, *129*

neon lighting *72*, *72*, 73, 87

Nicholas, Bill 19

Nicolson, Ben 86

nicotiana 19, 90

Noel, Anthony 62

Noguchi, Isamu 78

Norton, Judy 25

O

Oates, Christina 87

obelisks *30*, 77, 81, 105, 110

objets trouvés 6–7, 82

offices *114*, 129

orangeries 97

orchids 33

Osler, Mirabel 34, 38, *39*, *113*

Oudolf, Piet 106

outdoor showers 121

P

pagodas 29, 40, *32*

palms 20, 30, 33, 94

  king 19

  sago *22*, 25

pans *88*, 90

parterres 110, 133

passageways, latticed 29

passionflower vines 110

paths 6, 25, *25*, *26*, *35*, 37, *37*, 41, 48, *71*, 77, *80*, *113*, *126*, 131, 133, 134, 136

pavilions 29, *30*

paving 23, 27, 72, 124, *125*, 134, 136

pea gravel 133

pebbles *16*, 20, 41, *41*, 43, 49, 51, *51*, *71*, *72*, 84, *88*, *90*, 93, *98*, *116*, *120*, *123*, 127, *129*, 131, *131*, *132*, 133, 134

pedestals 33

pediments 33

pelargoniums 89

pepper trees *56*

perovskia *13*

phormium 12

pickets 101

pillows *19*, *20*

Plain Air *59*

plant supports, decorative 100–105

planters *26*, 27, *75*, 91, *92*, 97, 128, 134

plants

  annual 105

  flowering 20

  foliage *22*, *25*, 51, 90

  herbaceous 105

  potted 20, *20*, 25, *62*, *92*, *109*, *114*

  shade-loving 16

  silver-leaved *26*, *89*, *90*

  spiky *94*

  sun-loving 13

ponds *72*, 121, *123*, *123*

  container 97, 99

pools *16*, 19, 20, *22*, 25, 33, *45*, *72*, 99, *118*, 121, 122, *131*

poppies *59*

  plume *111*

potagers 23, *26*, *98*, 110

pots 13, 26, 33, *37*, *39*, *72*, 75, *83*, 84, 89–94, *97*, *98*, 106, *109*, 110, 114, *114*

Power, Nancy Goslee 16, 19, 20

pumps 122, 123

Pye, William 86

pyramids 110

R

rafters *20*

railway sleepers 128, *132*

Raven, Sarah *65*, *103*

Rawlinson, Mary *65*

red cedar 41, *41*, *128*, 131

Rheinstein, Suzanne 23

rocks 51, *79*, *79*

roof finials *39*

roof terraces 6, 40–45, 54, *55*, *72*, 98, *129*

rose arbours 58

rose bowers 54

rosemary 106, *111*

roses 38, *59*, *66*, *98*, *113*

  climbing *35*, *36*, 101–2, *101*, *104*, 116

  'Noisette Carnée' *36*

S

salvage *29*, 30, *30*, *32*, 79–80, *80*, 82, *84*, 91, 93

sandpit 44

sandstone 131

Schoellen, Marc *87*, *111*

Schwartz, Martha 78

screens *41*, *42*, 106

sculpture 6, 29, 30, *30*, *32*, 33, 44, 48, 71, 76–87

sea kale *39*

seating 15, 20, 34, *41*, 54–65

  built–in 16, *19*, 56

  stepped 19

  see also armchairs; chairs; daybeds; settles; sofas

sempervivums *93*, *94*

settles *65*, *113*

sheds *103*, 114, *116*

shells *93*, *94*

shelves 20, *20*, *39*, 98

shrines 87

shrubs 43, 94, 106

shutters *30*

Silva, Roberto 48, *135*

silver birch *41*, 43, 98

slate 49, 51, *51*, 58, 86, 124, *126*, *132*, 133–4, *135*

Smith, Joe *79*

sofas 6, 19, *19*, *20*, *59*

soil 93, 94, *94*

Solanum crispum 101

solariums *72*

Soleirolia soleirolii 127

spider plants 30, *32*, 33

spotlights *71*

squash 102

stairs *72*

  see also steps

stakes 101, 105

statues *11*, *29*, 82, *83*

stepped gables *117*

stepping stones *130*

steps *15*, 54, 67, *123*, 124, 128, *129*, *131*, *132*, 136, *136*

  see also stairs

stone *22*, 40, *41*, 43, 44, 49, 51, 77, *79*, 124, *129*, 133

  Cotswold 133

quarried 124, 127, 134
stones 7, 43–4, *49*, *97*, *102*, *121*, *132*
Storey, Sally *71*
strawberries 92
streams 72, 121, *121*
Strelitzia 136
succulents 27, *79*, *88*, *90*, *92*, *94*, *136*
"Sulking House," Bryan's Ground *117*
summerhouses 7, *30*, *32*, 38, 86, *112*, *114*, *117*
sundecks 54
sundials 86
Sutton Place 86
sweet peas *103*, *105*
swimming pools 23, *56*, *116*, 118, 121
swings 58, 65
T
tables 7, *15*, *37*, 54, *55*, 56, *68*, 86, 114
dining 71, *113*
glass-topped *56*, *92*
Japanese-style *77*
metal 62
mosaic 19, *20*, 56

painted *94*
pallet 12, *12*, 14
slate-topped 58
topiary *109*
tree trunk *59*
wooden *20*, 58, 65
Taggart, Nick *66*
Taxus baccata 106
tea glasses *15*, 68
teepees *103*
temples 29, *29*, *32*, 113
terraces *16*, 25, *25*, 48, 54, 56, 58, *77*, *88*, 127, *129*, *131*, 134, *135*, 136
tiles *92*
topiary 34, *37*, 38, *63*, *97*, 106–11
trash cans 13, *13*, *89*, 94
treehouses 7, 86
tree lights 6, *15*, 66, *66*, *68*, 72, 114
trees
avenue of 106
canopy *62*, 86, *101*
planting 94
trellis 11, *12*, *35*, *39*, 89, *102*, *129*
troughs *11*, *13*, *45*, *120*, 121

tubs 7, 91, 97, 128
tulips 90
Turrell, James 87
U
uplighters 14, *15*, 70, 71–2, *71*
urns *26*, *27*, *39*, *79*
V
vats 13, 97
vegetable patches 97, 99
vegetables 13
Verey, Rosemary 102
violets 75
votive candles *15*, *66*, 68, 74
W
walkways 29, *29*, 30, *32*, 86, 128
walls
brick *39*, *120*
concrete 19, *56*, *77*
curved 47, *47*, *51*, *79*
dry-laid stone 6, 48, 49, *51*, *79*, *135*
with glass *125*
loggia 19
and neon light 73
painted 11, 16, *16*, *19*
retaining *15*, 19, 20, 54, *83*, *123*, *124*, *127*, 134, *135*
slate 49, 51, *51*, *135*

washed *20*
water 40, 44, *45*, *49*, 67, 74, 86
water features 6, 7, 16, 72, 118–23, *131*
water lilies 19, 97, 99
water pumps 36
waterfalls *131*
watering cans 97, *98*
Wheeler, David *117*
Whitelaw, Lindsey 42
Whitelaw Turkington 42
wigwams, twiggy *103*, 105
willow 43, 102, 105
corkscrew *41*
Kilmarnock 38
wigwam 101
Wilson, Ben 86
wind chimes 7, *84*, 86
windbreaks 42
windowboxes *126*
windows 41, *41*, 114
double-hung 11
wood 40, 41, 44, 65, 77
Woodhams, Stephen *72*, *120*
Y
yew 106, 110

ACKNOWLEDGMENTS

We would like to thank all the garden owners and designers who so kindly opened their gardens to us and spent time with us on our visits: Mart Barlow, Jonathan Bell, Susan Berger and Helen Phillips, Riet Brinkhof and Joop Van Den Berk, Andrew Cao and Steven Jerrom, Nellie Christiaans and Manus Hijmans, Laura Cooper and Nick Taggart, the Farrell family, Isabelle Greene, Janey Hall, Sarah Harrison and Jamie Hodder-Williams, Ivan Hicks, Judy Horton, Jan Howard, Fiona Naylor, Peter Marlow and Lindsey Whitelaw, Judy Kameon, Dale Loth, Niall Manning and Alastair Morton, Lucy Moore, James Morris, Christina and Nigel Oates, Mirabel Osler, Nancy Goslee Power, Sarah Raven and Adam Nicolson, Suzanne Rheinstein, Marc Schoellen, Roberto Silva, Sally Storey, Tom Stuart-Smith and family, Carol Valentine, David Wheeler and Simon Dorrell, Hutton Wilkinson, Frank Wilson, Stephen Woodhams. A huge thank you also to Kay Acuragi and Frances Anderton for help with the American locations, and to everyone at Ryland Peters and Small, especially Clare Double, Sally Powell and, of course, Alison Starling who first approached us with the idea.

Elspeth Thompson and Melanie Eclare